ZODIAC SIGNS

♉ ♈ ♊ ♋ ♌ ♍

♎ ♏ ♐ ♑ ♒ ♓

ZODIAC SIGNS

FREDERICK GOODMAN

Brian Trodd Publishing House Limited

All photographs by Images Colour Library
(Leeds and London)

Published in 1990 by
Brian Trodd Publishing House Limited
27 Swinton Street, London WC1X 9 NW

ISNB 1 85361 077 1

Printed in Czechoslovakia

Contents

The Two Zodiacs

In a very general sense, there are two zodiacs, which are very different from each other, and which are related only in a communal imagery. The first, which is really the true zodiac, is an imaginary division of space into a band of twelve equal arcs, centred on the apparent path of the Sun: the other, which should not be called a zodiac at all, consists of twelve star-groups.

The zodiac proper is the division of the ecliptic (the imaginary path of the Sun, as seen from the Earth) into twelve equal arcs of 30 degrees each. This is the 'tropical'

zodiac, which is used by the majority of astrologers as the basis for their horoscopes. Figures 1 and 2, although from medieval astrological sources, reflect precisely the basic imagery of this twelve-figured tropical zodiac, which starts with the Ram of Aries, and completes the circuit with the Fishes of Pisces. Figure 1 is a 'flat' projection of the zodiac, which circles the Earth, while Figure 1a shows the same zodiac as it is conceived in three-dimensional form.

The complete order of the twelve signs is:

Aries the Ram

Taurus the Bull

Gemini the Twins

Cancer the Crab

Leo the Lion

Virgo the Virgin

Libra the Balance

Scorpio the Scorpion

Sagittarius the Archer

Capricorn the Goat-fish

Aquarius the Water-bearer

Pisces the Fishes.

While there are sometimes important and even significant deviations from these associations (for example, Capricorn is not always a goat-fish, for it is sometimes portrayed as a goat), the general imagery listed above is found in almost all zodiacal figures from classical times.

The second zodiac is not a zodiac in the true sense of the word, though it is often called the 'constellational zodiac'. This star-zodiac consists of twelve images,

1. The twelve images of the zodiac in circular sequence, from an early sixteenth-century woodcut.

1a. A sixteenth-century hand-coloured woodcut showing personification of Astrology (left) and the most famous astronomer of ancient times, Ptolemy, beneath a model of the celestial sphere, with the zodiacal band around the Earth.

2. The twelve images of the zodiac surrounded by the twelve corresponding houses. The central concentrics show the Earth (in the medieval cosmology, the cosmic system was geocentric) and the seven planets. From a print after Leonard Reymanns, 1555.

fancifully traced in the pattern of stars, and given the same order, and the same names, as the twelve in the tropical zodiac. The important thing about this zodiac is that the twelve figures do not fit into arcs of the same length, nor are they all disposed within the ecliptic band. The two-colour constellational map in Figure 3 is designed around a chart drawn by the German artist Albrecht Dürer in 1515 – the twelve

3. A woodcut of northern constellations, including the zodiacal constellations, designed by Dürer in 1515, according to the calculations of Heinfogel and Stabius.

4. Classical constellation figure, as reproduced by the Renaissance printer Aldus, with (*4a* opposite) the twelve zodiacal asterisms separated.

constellations picked out in colour indicate those star-groups which have the same names as those in the tropical zodiac. We note that some of these images are quite lárge, while some are relatively small. A much older map of the stars, visualized as constellation images, is that reproduced by the Renaissance printer Aldus (Fig. 4) from which it is easily possible to identify the twelve constellation images (Fig. 4a).

As further examples, we may take the two constellation maps in Figures 5 and 6, which were designed by astronomers living almost 250 years apart, yet which clearly show that the areas occupied by the twelve 'constellational images' are much the same in both cases, relative to the size of the map itself. There is little or no relationship between these two constellational 'zodiacs' and the equal-arc zodiac of Figure 2.

The difference between the two zodiacs is expressed in yet another comparison, which is the basic astrological charts of Figures 7 and 8, the former of which represents a tropical zodiac, the latter a constellational chart. The twelve equal-arc sections (here represented by symbols called 'sigils') which denote the twelve images (Fig. 7), are disposed in 30 degree arcs, and are properly called 'signs'. The constellational zodiac (Fig. 8), here traced out as imaginary trace-lines between stars in the relevant area of the sky, are properly called 'constellations' – more precisely, 'constellational zodiac images'. The confusion between the signs and the constellations, while common in non-specialist minds, should not really arise, for the signs relate to the zodiac, while the constellational images relate to the patterns of stars. A useful diagram,

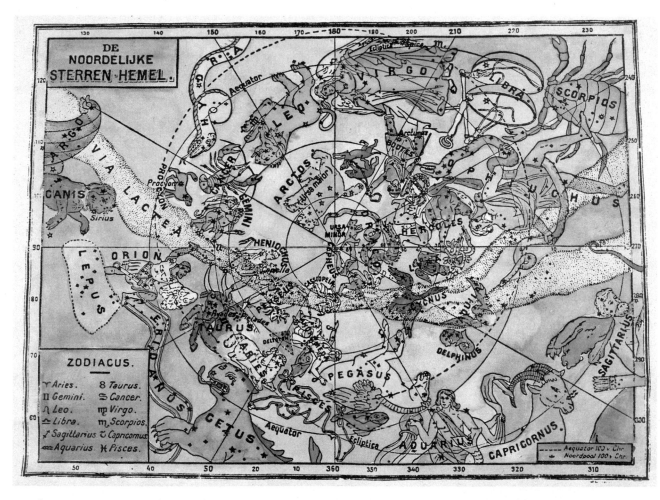

5 (opposite). Constellation map of the eighteenth century, printed for Gerald Valk and Peter Schenk.

6. Dutch constellation map, as reproduced by 'Libra' in *Astrology. Its Technics and Ethics*, 1917.

setting out a comparison of four arcs of the tropical zodiac, alongside the corresponding constellational images, is given in Figure 9. This shows the last four divisions of the equal-sign zodiac, in backwards order from Pisces to Sagittarius. Below, in the corresponding equal arcs, are set out the patterns of the star-groups traced by astronomers in the sky. Just below the equatorial line (EQ) we see the complex pattern of stars forming Aquarius (AQ), which is set in the first third of zodiacal Pisces, and throws its arm into the last two-thirds of zodiacal Aquarius. The con-

stellation Capricorn (CP) is bunched up in the first two-thirds of zodiacal Aquarius, while Sagittarius (SG) occupies the full extent of Capricorn. Strangest of all, in some respects, is the existence of a non-zodiacal constellation, Ophiuchus, actually touching the ecliptic line (EC) above the small constellation of Scorpius (SC). The proximity of Ophiuchus to the ecliptic indicates that there are more constellations along the ecliptic belt than merely twelve – this in itself should indicate the profound difference between the equal-arced tropical zodiac, and the circle of unequal asterisms,

13

7. Diagram of the tropical zodiac of equal-arc signs, the zodiacal areas marked by the symbols for the signs, which are technically called 'sigils'.

stellational zodiac in their horoscopes, the majority of astrological practice involves the tropical zodiac.

While the constellational zodiac is used only rarely by most modern astrologers, the influences of the stars (some of which are, of course, set in the constellational zodiac images) are often taken into account in horoscopic interpretation. A rich body of knowledge, mainly derived from Arabian astrology, has been preserved relating to the meaning and influences of individual stars when these are, for one reason or another, emphatic in a personal chart. Sometimes the qualities ascribed to the individual stars are reflected in the supposed nature, or mythology, of the figure into which they have been imaginatively integrated. At other times, the stars have a significance quite separate from the asterism in which they are located.

To modern eyes, the derivation of images of animals, humans and objects from star groups appears to be too imaginative or poetic to have much real significance. Why, one might ask, should an astronomer trace in the pattern of stars in Figure 11 the image of a giant holding a club and a cloak? The question is a valid one, but it is likely that the reason for tracing such a figure in that part of the skies has nothing to do with the pattern of the stars themselves, but rather with the stream of spiritual influence which the ancients imagined came from that part of the skies.

For a variety of historical reasons, the two 'zodiacs', of the tropical and stellar kind, have different traditions attached to them, and both of these are of importance to any study of the zodiac. The literature relating to the star-groups usually contains many pictures of different constellation

or star-figures in the constellational charts.

In astrology both the tropical zodiac and the constellational figures are used, though for different purposes. In most cases, the astrologer will use the tropical zodiac as the basis for his chart – we may see this from a comparison between a personal horoscope, that cast by the astrologer Pearce for the British King George V (Fig. 10) and the diagram of the signs and sigils in the tropical zodiac of Figure 1. While some astrologers do make use of the con-

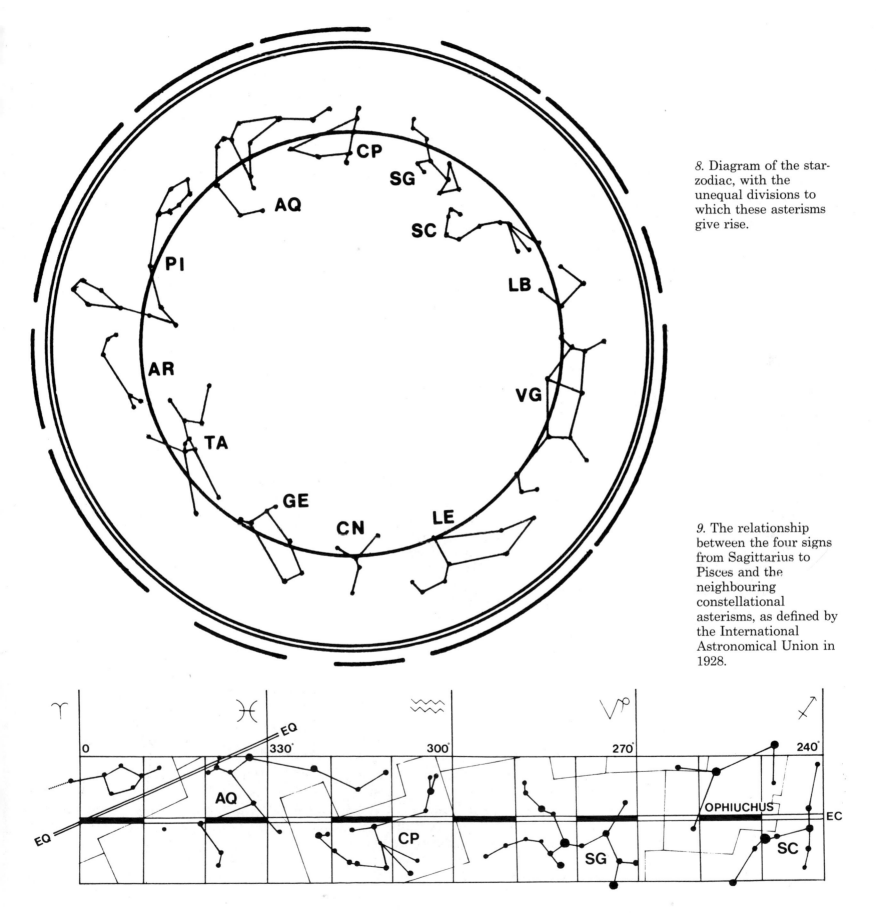

8. Diagram of the star-zodiac, with the unequal divisions to which these asterisms give rise.

9. The relationship between the four signs from Sagittarius to Pisces and the neighbouring constellational asterisms, as defined by the International Astronomical Union in 1928.

15

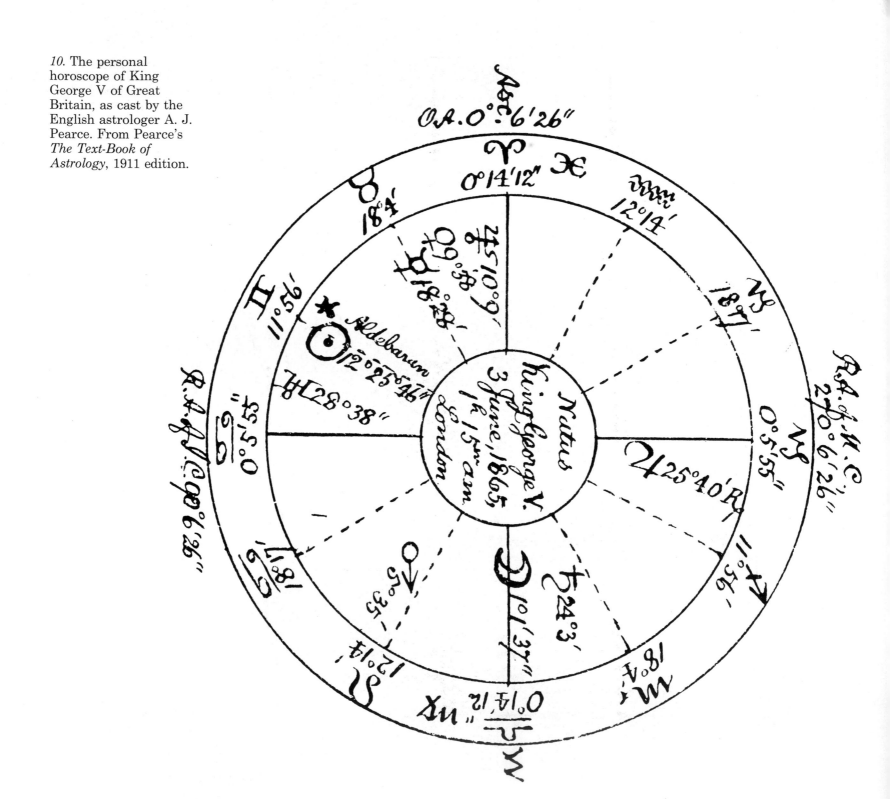

10. The personal horoscope of King George V of Great Britain, as cast by the English astrologer A. J. Pearce. From Pearce's *The Text-Book of Astrology*, 1911 edition.

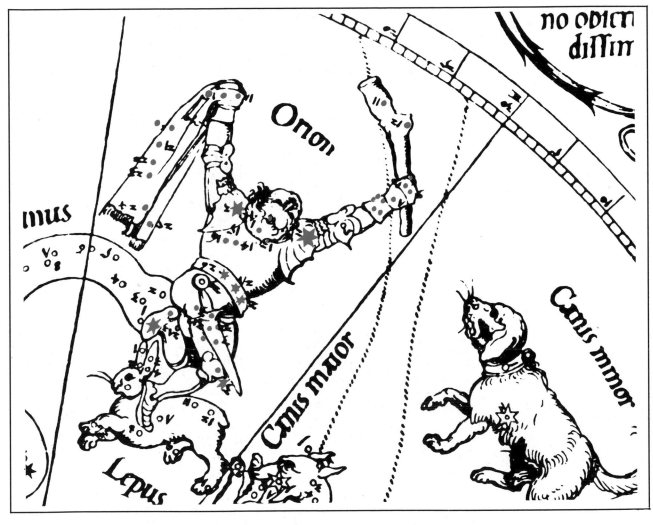

images, studded with stars, as for example in the beautiful image of Aries the Ram in Figure 27, or in the splendid Arabian constellational map in Figure 12, which portrays the zodiacal twelve only partially, on the very edge of the circumference. The texts accompanying such images are often in the form of poetry, telling stories of the genesis of these stellar images in forms which may be traced back to the mythology of ancient Greek times, or even earlier. More often than not, this mythology weaves together esoteric and exoteric accounts of how particular star-groups were formed by the gods, when the spiritual beings had a much closer relationship to human beings, in former times: the star-maps, therefore, are almost the equivalent of pagan books of Genesis.

We learn, for example, from such stories that the band of cloud-like stars which we now call the Milky Way (clearly defined in the stretch of clouds in the map of Fig. 6) was said to have been created when the

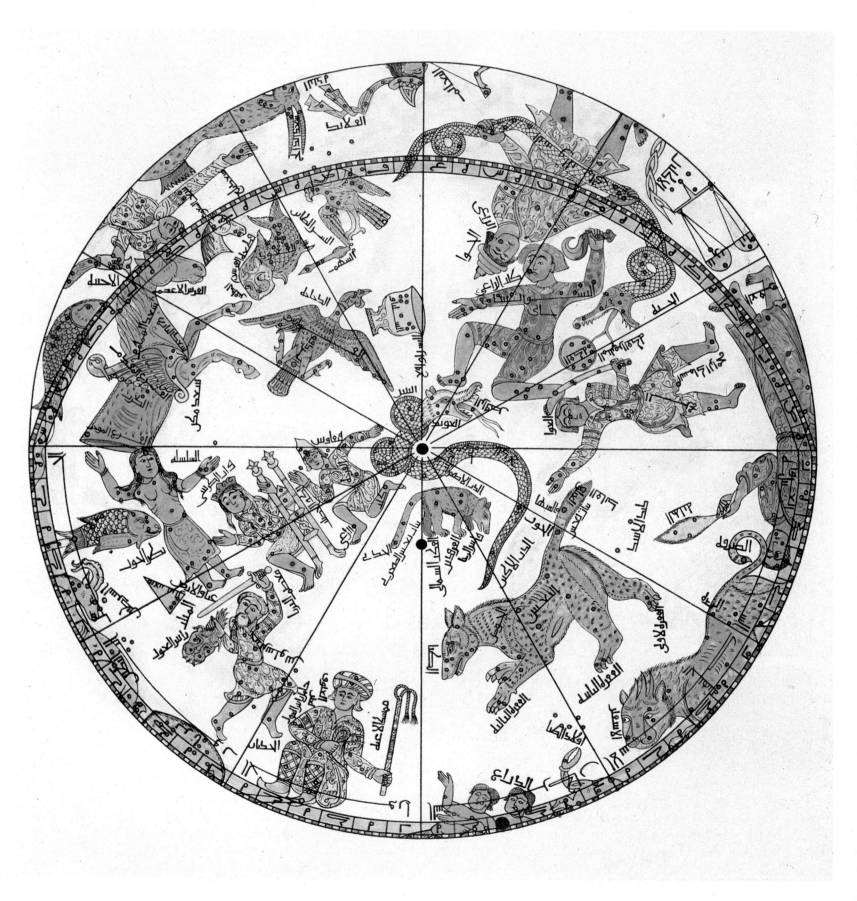

18

child Hercules sucked too fiercely at the breasts of the goddess Hera. The milk which squirted upwards, into the heavens, became the Milky Way, while that which squirted to the Earth made the white lilies. The woodcut from Natalis Comitis' *Mythologiae* of 1616 (Fig. 13) illustrates this making of the Milky Way, by depicting the milk which streams from the mouth of the child already formed into the band of the Way, with the drips creating the lilies below. In another version of the myth, we learn that the god Saturn, wishing as always to devour his children (he being the god of Time, among other things), was given a stone in place of

one of the babies, and would have choked to death had his wife not poured milk down his throat. The milk which overflowed formed the present Milky Way. Such stories, while appearing simple, and even empty of sense, are usually filled with secret meanings, relating to the nature of the corresponding stellar groups, the zodiacal signs and the planets. Indeed, an impressive literature has been established through the ages in attempts to explain and understand these impressive stories.

Frequently such mythology is designed to hide meanings about the sacred temple-lore, which was, in former times, expressed

12 (opposite). Arabian constellation figure, with the images of the twelve constellational figures on the very edge of the circle – note the two fishes to the left of the circle, and the back of the lion to the bottom right. After a lithograph by Nethercote, *c.* 1890.

13. The Origin of the Milky Way – a woodcut from Natalis Comitis' *Mythologiae*, printed at Pavia in 1616, showing Hercules sucking at the breast of the sleeping Hera with such force that her stream of milk forms the Milky Way, and the lilies.

14. A comparison between the images derived from the ancient Egyptian zodiac and a modern series. The image for Virgo in the Egyptian zodiac is a form of the goddess Isis, holding what was later interpreted as an ear of corn. By the late nineteenth century the Christian 'Madonna' imagery had so pervaded the sign that Virgo was often portrayed in the guise of Queen of Heaven. 'Queen of Heaven' was actually one of the titles of the Egyptian Isis.

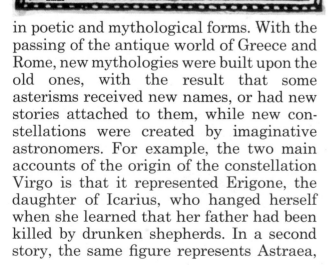

14a. Images from a modern zodiac of Leo, Virgo, Cancer and Sagittarius.

in poetic and mythological forms. With the passing of the antique world of Greece and Rome, new mythologies were built upon the old ones, with the result that some asterisms received new names, or had new stories attached to them, while new constellations were created by imaginative astronomers. For example, the two main accounts of the origin of the constellation Virgo is that it represented Erigone, the daughter of Icarius, who hanged herself when she learned that her father had been killed by drunken shepherds. In a second story, the same figure represents Astraea,

the starry daughter of one of the giant Titans, who took the part of the gods when they went to war against these ancient giants, and therefore betrayed her father. The early Christians ignored both these Greek myths, and adapted for their own symbolic purposes the ancient Egyptian mythology, which had traced in the same stars the image of the goddess Isis (see Figs. 14 and 14a), her dress flowing with stars, and either a wand of office or the child Horus in her arms. They turned this image into the Virgin Mary (Fig. 15), postulating that the sign opposite to Virgo, the Fishes of

15 (right). Wood engraving of the Virgin Mary, with her robe covered in ears of corn. These ears of corn have their origin in the imagery of the Egyptian goddess Isis.

16 (opposite). 'Faelis, the Cat' from the 1805 edition of Lalande's *Bibliographie Astronomique*.

Pisces, was her child Jesus, who became the Christ.

A striking example of the creation of a new constellational image from supposed star-patterns is that of Faelis, The Cat (Fig. 16), which was formed in the skies by Lalande at the beginning of the nineteenth century, from a group of stars between Antlia (the Air Pump) and Hydra (the Water Snake). 'The starry sky has worried me quite enough in my life,' wrote the old astronomer, after forming this image, 'so now I can have my joke with it'. His joke did not last long, however, for the asterism was never widely adopted by other astronomers, and has now been forgotten, save by historians.

These different mythologies and the accretion of newly developed asterisms overlapped, and created deep levels of meaning which were expressed in hundreds of different poems and images, all of which contributed to the growth of astrological lore. We shall note one or two interesting examples of how this mythology is related to secret meanings when we examine in some depth the traditions still attached to the twelve signs. The surviving fragments of the old mythologies indicate that the ancients were prepared to read the imaginary star-groups as though the whole of the sky were a book, which told the complicated story of how the gods and goddesses related to the world in which men lived.

While there are only twelve signs of the zodiac, there are a large number of constellational images, the actual number depending upon who designed a particular sky map, and upon the period upon which it was designed. In modern times well over a hundred distinct figures are traced in the

23

17. Classical constellation map, after Georg Thiele's *Antike Himmelsbilder*, Berlin, 1898.

changed to any significant extent in at least two thousand years.

The associations of the twelve signs of the zodiac are not themselves directly linked with the ancient mythologies, though the fact that the two zodiacs have shared the same names for so long has meant that during that period the poetic constellational stories have become inextricably bound up with the zodiacal traditions. In contrast to the mythological and mythopoetic lore of the constellations, the traditions of the twelve signs are related to astrological literature mainly in terms of their effects on man. The result is that there is an important corpus of astrological tradition which sets out the 'meanings' of the twelve signs in terms of character, temperaments, physical appearance, associate colours, associate gem-stones, sacred images, places, countries, cities, animals and so on. In fact, it is unlikely that in ancient times there was anything in the created world which was not regarded as having some distinct link with a zodiacal or planetary influence. There are a great many variant traditions but little agreement among astrologers as to which associations are the correct ones.

The creature most 'explained' in terms of zodiacal associations was Man himself. Each person was regarded as being under the rule of a single zodiacal sign, which was determined by the degree of the zodiac arising over the horizon at the moment of his or her birth. Each person was accorded a different 'zodiacal gem' which could be worn to avert dark occult powers, or attract the beneficial influences of his or her own zodiacal 'star'. The destiny of each person was seen and understood in terms of the entire 'horoscope' figure, which set out in

skies, but in ancient times the sky map was more simple, with fewer than 50 images clearly defined, as the classical constellational map in Figure 17 indicates. In fact, it is instructive to examine this map carefully, and attempt to trace the twelve images of the constellational zodiac, if only to see the extent to which these have not

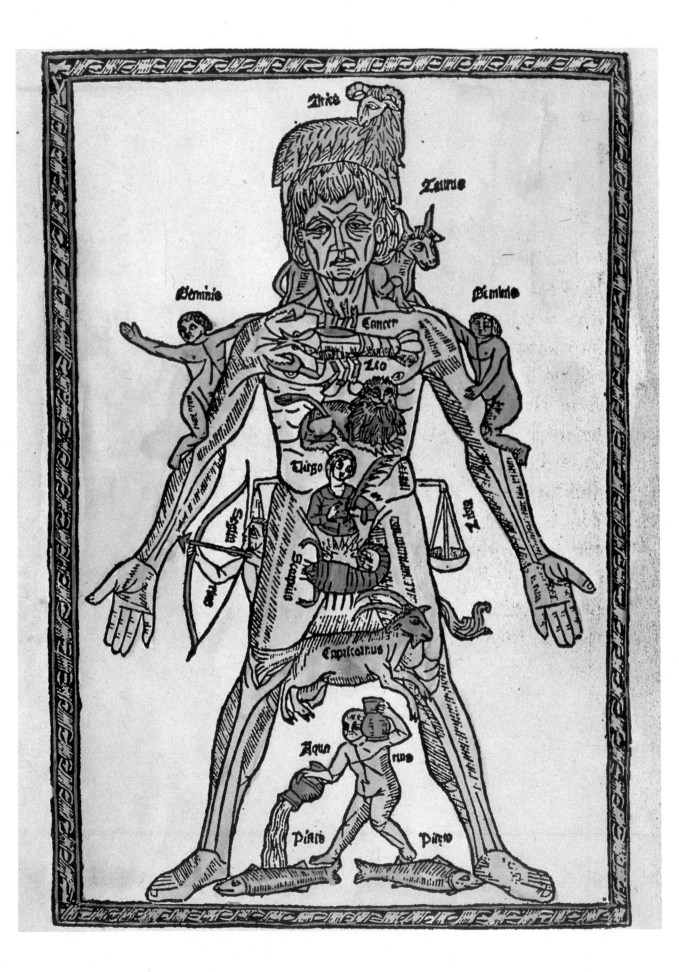

18. Melothesic figure, from a sixteenth-century Shepherd's Calendar.

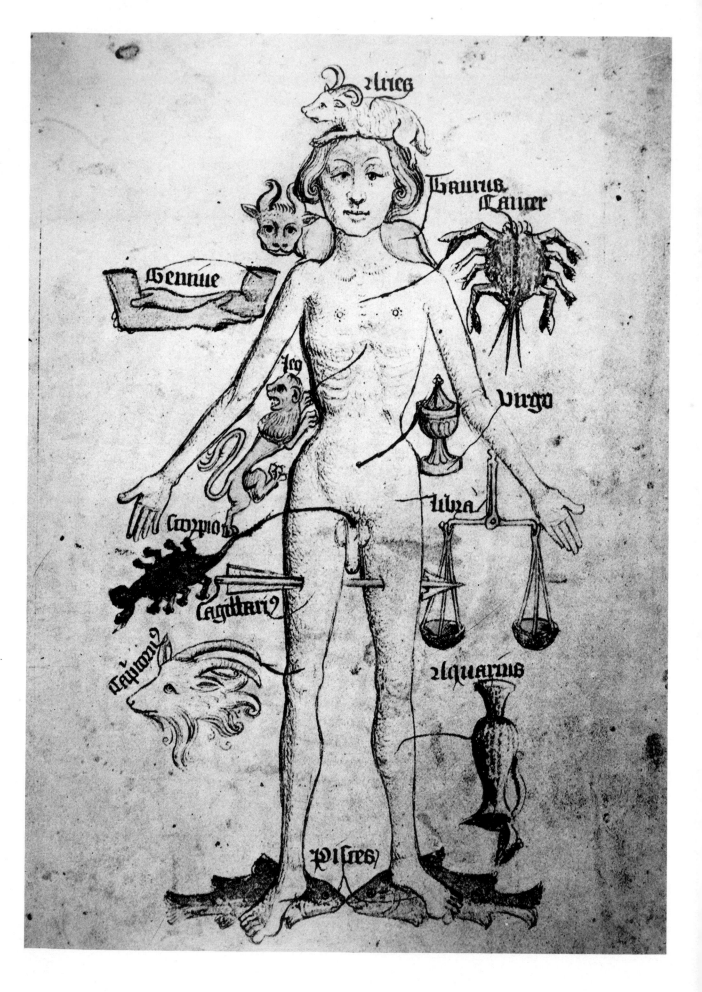

19 (right). Melothesic figure, from the sixteenth-century *The Guildbook of the Barber Surgeons of York* in the British Library, London.

20 (opposite). Pagan-classical melothesic image, drawn in the early twelfth century but based on a classical model, with a personification of the Sun at the centre and the parts of the body linked (in the inscription) with the corresponding twelve images. The figures on the outside of the circle represent the four seasons. Copy after the original in the Bibliothèque Nationale, Paris.

diagramatic form the positions of the zodiac, the planets, the twelve houses, and so on. Above all, each person was represented in terms of what has since been called a melothesic figure, the 'zodiacal man', which portrays the supposed or real influences of the twelve signs on the body of man (Figs. 18 and 19).

Although the literary tradition was known from the writings of the Roman astrologer Ptolemy long before the twelfth century, these melothesic drawings, based on Ptolemy's own observations, did not enter the West until some time in the early twelfth century – though in modern times earlier, pagan examples of drawings showing the relationship between the human body and the twelve signs have been discovered (Fig. 20). These diagrams came to the West by way of the Arabian literature, the astrological lore of which was highly sophisticated. The early Byzantine melothesic man (Fig. 21) sets out the planetary and zodiacal influences on different parts of the body, but since the sigils used to denote the planets, and a few of the zodiacal signs, are medieval, it is not easy for someone unversed in the astrological traditional to read them. However, the signs represented by these sigils do correspond almost exactly to the list of signs set out for the zodiacal man in Figure 22, which was drawn up by an Italian astrologer a few hundred years later. This tradition is still in use in modern astrology, though it is now realized by many astrologers that there is a hidden meaning in the ancient lore, and the melothesic figure is not quite so simple as has been imagined in former times. It is now appreciated that the imagery refers to the 'inner man' as well as to the outer body – that, for example, the

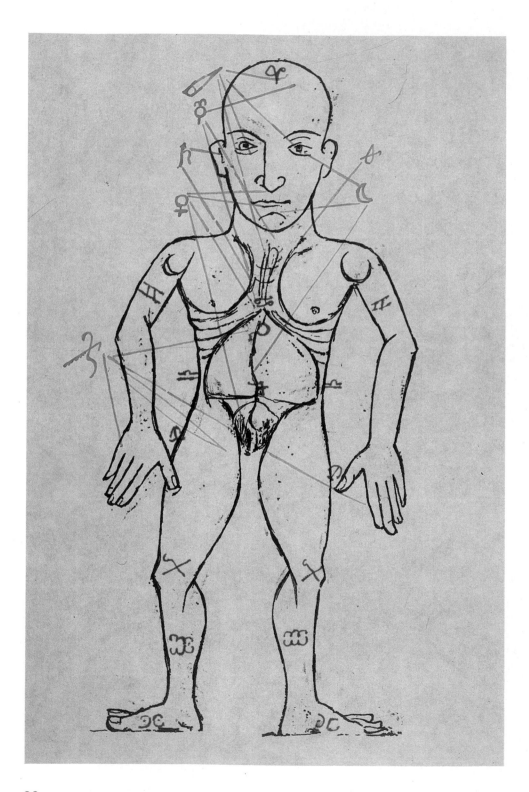

rulership of Aries is more than merely an influence over the head, but over the inner activity of the head, where thought and imagination is born: the Aries type is quick to plunge into action because (by nature) he or she does not distinguish thinking from action – to think is to act. The inner correspondences of the melothesic figure apply to each of the other zodiacal rulerships over the body, though not all of them are immediately apparent.

One very important part of the astrological tradition which is frequently observed in the melothesic figures, as indeed in early horoscopes, is that connected with the use of sigils – the graphic symbols intended to represent the planets, signs of the zodiac, and other astrological factors, samples of which we have already noted in Figure 21. The twelve sigils for the signs of the zodiac are beautifully portrayed in the alchemical diagram of Figure 23, and although this design was made in the seventeenth century, a modern astrologer would have no difficulty in recognizing them even today. With a little care, a non-astrologer should be able to work out which of the sigils in the horoscope chart in Figure 10 corresponds to the twelve of Figure 23. The further one goes back in time, however, the less the zodiacal and planetary sigils resemble the familiar ones in use today. Almost all the sigils around the magical diagram of Figure 24 closely resemble the modern sigils (that for Sagittarius is a notable exception, as is the one for Pisces). This diagram was constructed at the end of the fifteenth century. A further two centuries back, however, the sigils are scarcely recognizable, as the reconstructed horoscope in Figure 25, based on a thirteenth-century chart, indicates. This horoscope,

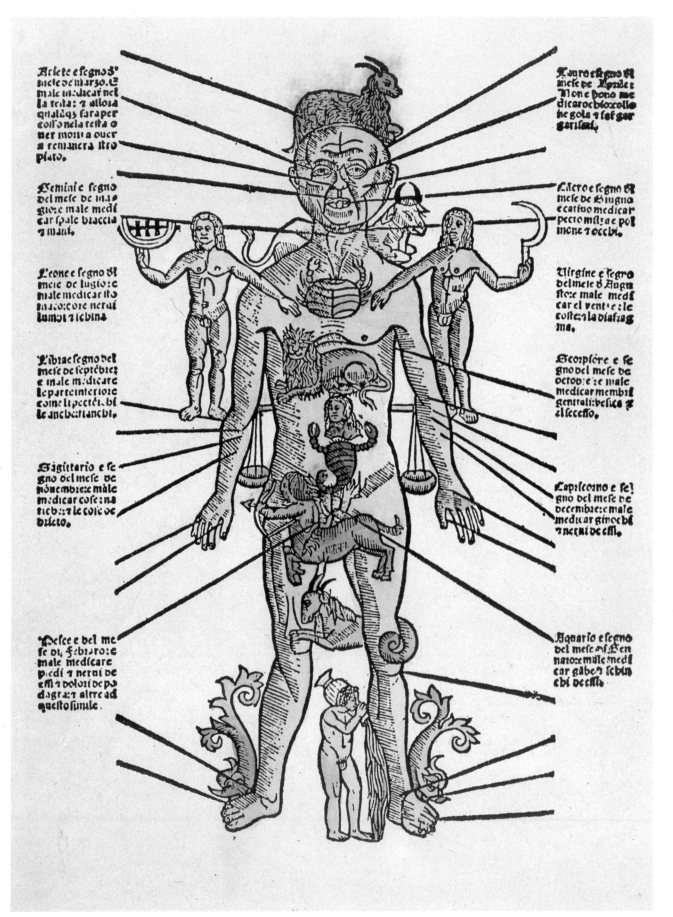

Arete e fegno 3º
mefe de marzo. e
male medicar nel
la tefta: z alloza
qualuqz fara per
coffo nela tefta o
uer mozza ouer
a remanera lfo
piato.

Geminie fegno
del mefe de mag
gioze male medi
car fpale biaccia
z mani.

L'eone e fegno el
mefe de luglio: e
male medicar lfo
mazo:core nerui
lumoz z la bina

Libza e fegno del
mefe de feptebze
e male medicare
le parte inferioze
come li peccti: bi
le anebantiancbi.

Gagittario e fe
gno del mefe de
nouembze: e male
medicar cofe: na
ticbe: z le cofe de
dzicto.

Pefce e del me
fe de febzaro: e
male medicare
piedi z nerui de
effi z dolozi de po
dagra: z altre ad
quefto fimile.

Tauro e fegno el
mefe de apzile e
none bono me
dicar oe bi occollo
be gola z faf gar
gatifmi.

Lifcro e fegno el
mefe de Giugno
e cattuo medicar
pecto mifza e pol
mone z occbi.

Uirgine e fegno
del mefe d'Augu
fto e male medi
car el vente: le
cofte: z la diafzag
ma.

Scozpfore e fe
gno del mefe de
octobze: e male
medicar membzi
genitali: befica z
el feceffo.

Capzicozno e fe
gno del mefe de
decembze: e male
medicar ginocbi
z nerui de effi.

Aquario e fegno
del mefe of Gen
nazo: e male medi
car gabe: z febin
cbi de effi.

cast for 12 May 1203, contains a number of zodiacal sigils which few modern astrologers would be able to read (that for Libra, in the bottom left section, is an exception). The origin of these magical sigils is almost a story in itself, but we shall note some of the interpretations accorded the zodiacal sigils in the individual sections dealing with the twelve images.

23 (opposite). The twelve zodiacal sigils, from the 1677 edition of the alchemical text Aureus Tractatus.

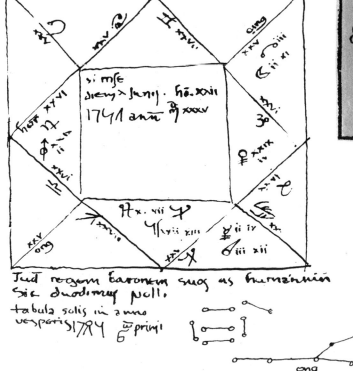

24 (above). Magical image with the twelve zodiacal sigils, from the 1530 edition of Agrippa's *De Occulta Philosophia.*

25 (left). Thirteenth-century sigils and abbreviations on a horoscope figure: composite copy from contemporaneous horoscopes in the British Library, London.

31

The Twelve Personalities

In the astrological tradition, the 'personalities' of those born under the various signs have been given a great deal of attention. The following brief digest sets out the main traditions.

Aries has an assertive nature, a drive towards individuality, and the conscious aim of establishing energetic leadership.

Taurus has a conservative, rather fixed nature, a drive towards possessiveness, and a conscious aim involved with the realization of material security.

Gemini has a quick, changeable nature, a drive towards a versatile development of self-awareness, and a conscious aim involved with establishing intellectual communication with others.

Cancer has a retiring, moody nature, a drive towards establishing romantic attachments, and a conscious aim involved with the sensitive unfolding of a rich emotional life.

Leo has an exuberant and proud nature, a drive towards vivifying experiences or creativity, and a conscious aim involved with dignified self-expression.

Virgo has a conscientious practical nature, a drive towards thoroughness in service, and a conscious aim involved with establishing just principles of order.

Libra has a gentle, discriminative nature, a drive towards the enjoyment of harmony, and a conscious aim involved with establishing stability and beauty in the environment.

Scorpio has an intense, strong-willed nature, a drive towards regeneration, and a conscious aim involved with the exercise of power – usually over others.

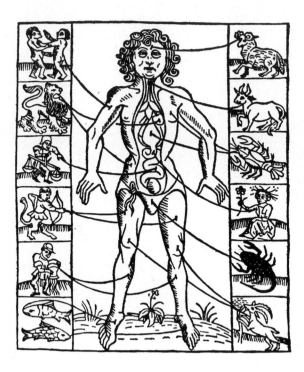

26. Twelve representations of the zodiacal images on a zodiacal man, from a medieval print in *Martyrologium der Heiligen nach dem Kalender*, 1484.

Sagittarius has a dignified, restless nature, a drive towards the exploration of ideas, and a conscious aim involved with the attainment of wisdom through experience.

Capricorn has a cautious though ambitious nature, a drive towards the practical expression of duty, and a conscious aim involved with being useful and dependable.

Aquarius has an unconventional, humanitarian nature, a drive towards a detached, if original, pursuit of truth, and a conscious aim involved with the expression of useful knowledge.

Pisces has an imaginative, highly emotional nature, a drive towards the sympathetic understanding of others, and a conscious aim involved with the search for emotional balance.

♈ ARIES

The standard image is that of the Ram (Fig. 27), and popular astrological texts usually point out that the Arietan personality tends to 'butt' people with its imaginary horns – usually to get his or her own way. The zodiac is a circle, and circles have neither beginning nor end, yet the convention that the zodiac begins with Aries, the leader of the herd of zodiacal creatures, appears to be as old as the zodiac itself. The oldest surviving name for Aries, relating to Assyrian astrology, means 'Prince', so we presume that the sign was regarded as a leader even at the beginning of history.

The modern sigil for Aries (Fig. 28) is said to be a vestigial drawing of the horns of the ram, but other authorities claim that it is a simple drawing of a fount of energy – which is certainly more representative of the personality of Aries than the image of a Ram. Another explanation for the symbol is that it is intended to represent a human face, being a vestigial drawing of the nose and the eyebrows. This is a fairly reasonable

27. Medieval constellational image of Aries the Ram, curiously painted with a blue body which has no relationship to the traditional colours of Aries. From a fifteenth-century astrological manuscript in the British Library, London.

JN forma anetis sit stelle. 13. ex quibꝪ due sn̄t de magnitudīe ma. ꝫ de

28 (right). The medieval sigil alongside the zodiacal image. The sigil for Aries is usually drawn as double curvature, expressive of an upward flow of energy. From an *Astrorum Scientia* of 1489.

29 (opposite left). Image of Aries from a late fifteenth-century edition of Albumasar.

30 (opposite right). Aries roundel from the thirteenth-century marble floor in Canterbury cathedral.

theory, since Aries has rule over the head and face in the traditional images of the zodiacal man in which the Ram is draped over the cranium or headgear of the cosmic man (Fig. 32). In terms of the magical symbolism, this particular view of the Ram in close proximity with the head relates to the peculiar power within Aries, which permits it to retain contact with the spiritual realm (visualized as being 'above' the human being, hovering invisibly in space). The process of 'thinking', or of any creative activity, is essentially the process of Aries in every human being, and some

astrologers have claimed that the symbol is not really a drawing of a fount of energy so much as the descent of spirit, from the vast reservoir of the higher spiritual realm, into the point above man's head, pointing to the fact that human thinking and creative activity is initiated in the brain.

Aries belongs to the Fire element – it is outgoing, pioneering, courageous, self-reliant, idealistic, enthusiastic and exaggerative. There is usually a strong selfishness, and a certain lack of sensitivity to the needs of others: under certain circumstances it may be overbearing, argumentative and coarse.

Designers of zodiacs usually emphasize the curvature of the horns when they draw the image of Aries (Fig. 29), but, on the whole, the images for Aries are relatively conservative in European astrology, as the selection of images from Canterbury and Ferrara in Figures 30 and 31 reveal, and as the whole sequence of images in Figure 32 indicates. A puzzling exception is the image of Aries among the zodiacal roundels on the tympanum of the Madeleine at Vezelay

31. Fifteenth-century fresco of Aries from the Palazzo Schifanoia, Ferrara.

(Fig. 33), which portrays Aries (and, for that matter, Taurus) with a fish-tail. The explanation for this curious deviation from the standard classical imagery is almost certainly that the fish-tailed Ram was depicted in some now-lost Arabian as-

trological manuscript, which certainly influenced other details of the Vezelay zodiacal imagery.

The ancient Egyptian zodiac from Denderah (Fig. 34) shows the ram in a pose which is not characteristic of the later

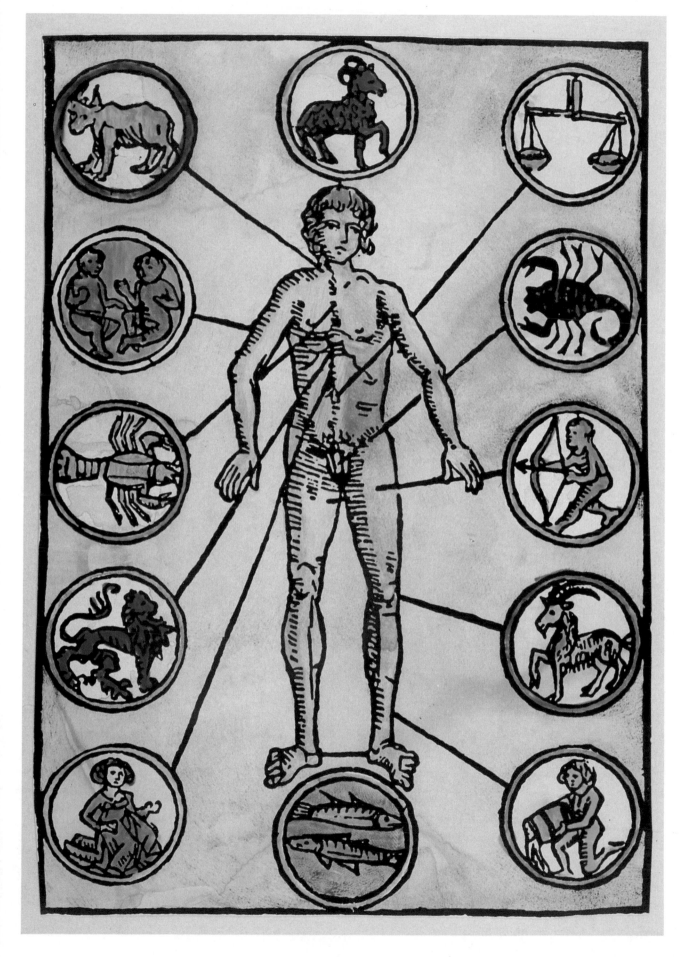

32. Aries (top) as ruler of the head – after a medieval image showing the human being in relation to the rulership of the twelve zodiacal signs.

33 (right). Roundels from the zodiacal belt on the tympanum of the narthex door of the Madeleine at Vezelay. Depicted in the top detail is the image of a fish-tailed Aries, and in the bottom detail the image of a fish-tailed Taurus.

34 (opposite). The Egyptian constellation map from the Temple of Hathor at Denderah, which has been dated to the first century of our era, but which appears to contain information of a much older type.

35. The syncretic zodiac of Kircher, which represents an attempt to relate zodiacal traditions to ancient mythological lore. In this highly imaginative interpretation, the sigil for Aries is derived from the horns of the Egyptian god Amun.

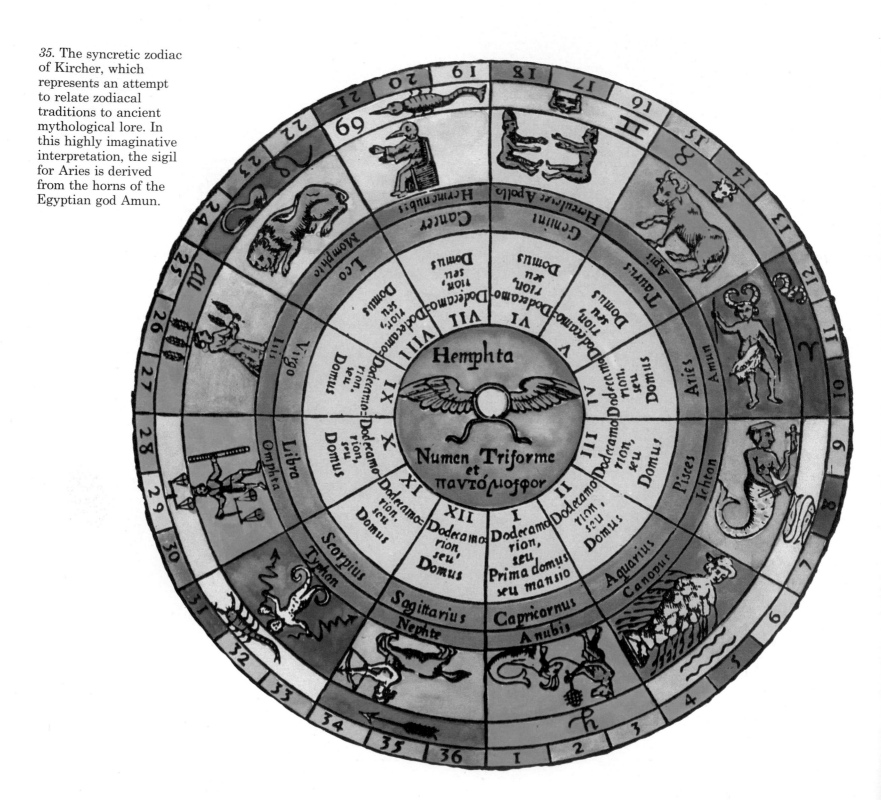

imagery. The Ram is lying down, and looking behind itself, rather than forward, with the anticipation proper to the Aries type. The horns of this Egyptian figure are intended to recall the horns of the god Amun, and this was a point developed by the polymath Athanasius Kircher when he constructed his own mythological zodiac (Fig. 35). Kircher proposes that the symbol for Aries is indeed a clumsy drawing of the horns of the ram – or, indeed, of the horns of Amun, whom he links directly with the sign as its mythological equivalent. It is interest-

ing that to this day the remains of the great temple of Amun at Thebes is approached by way of an avenue of ram-headed beasts (Fig. 36). In his role as Amon-Ra he was more than a sun-god, but actually the 'creator of the universe', and at one time the greatest deity of the Egyptians, the leader of all the other gods. In these associations we see something of the power of the spiritual realm reflected in the leader of the zodiacal herd, in a sign which relates to that time of the year when life is, so to speak, recreated anew.

36. The avenue of ram-headed beasts, creatures of Amun, lining the old sacred way to the temple complex at Thebes.

Zodiacal Fresco Cycles

In medieval times astrology became such an important aspect of the intellectual life that vast programmes were put in hand to represent astrological lore in architecture and painting – often in public buildings. Among the most impressive of the pictorial cycles are those found in Italy, in Padua, Ferrara, Vicenza and Rome.

The Paduan cycle is certainly one of the most ambitious of all frescoes, for within the Palazzo della Ragione, in a series of three registers, are over 217m (712ft) of fresco paintings relating to zodiacal, planetary, stellar and hermetic lore. There are over 333 separate compartments of images, some of which were said to have been painted originally by Giotto, following the stellar lore of the medieval astrologer Peter of Abano. However, fire damage in 1426, and later cyclone damage, in 1756, have resulted in large-scale restorations, so that it is no longer possible to trace for sure the styles of even the post-1420 painters, who were known to be Nicolo Mireti and Stefano de Ferrara. In spite of this, the cycle is still the most complex surviving example of an astrological programme, and while some

of the images are recognizable to the modern visitor – as for example the image of Capricorn (Fig. 39) – some of the symbolism is so arcane that its true meaning has been lost (Fig. 38).

37 (right). Fresco of Aries, from the Palazzo Schifanoia, Ferrara. Fifteenth-century design.

38 (above right). An unidentifiable symbol of fifteenth-century design, from the Salone, Padua.

39 (far right). Fresco of Capricorn, from the Salone, Padua. Fifteenth-century design.

The cycle of paintings in the Palazzo Schifanoia, in Ferrara, has not wholly survived, yet what is left points to a most erudite programme of astrological lore relating not to the zodiac (as is often believed) but to the decanates, which are the three-fold divisions of the zodiacal arcs, into arcs of 10 degrees. These decanates have been accorded a rich symbolism in traditional astrology, and it is this which we see preserved in the surviving frescoes (Figs. 37 and 40).

In Rome, the most impressive of the zodiacal cycles is that in the Chigi Palace, in the Farnesian, which is intended to represent the personal horoscope for 1 December 1466 of Agostino Chigi, the imagery representing a constellational horoscope rather than the more usual tropical kind.

The Vicenza series is much later than any of those in Padua, Ferrara or Rome, for it was painted in the sixteenth century by Domenico Rizzo. This remarkable fresco is the huge ceiling known as the 'Chiericati Firmamento', in the Palazzo of the same name, which is a highly organized sequence of constellational images around a central picture of Apollo and Diana, representatives of the Sun and Moon, in their chariots. There are over 80 identifiable constellations (Figs. 41 and 42) ranged in 77 separate fresco areas, separated by bands of plaster moulding which are themselves painted with cosmological and astrological imagery. Modern scholars have shown that the imagery of this Firmamento is largely derived from the zodiacal and constellational imagery of ancient Roman coinage-design, with many references to the famous Dürer constellational map of 1515 (Fig. 3).

40 (far left). Detail of a mysterious man holding a circle and a rod – symbols of spirit and matter respectively. This is one of the decanate images for the zodiacal images in the Palazzo Schifanoia, Ferrara. Fifteenth century.

41 (far left bottom). Fresco of Andromeda, chained to the rock, from the Chiericati Firmamento, Vicenza. Sixteenth century.

42 (left). Fresco of Pisces, Aquarius and Sagittarius, from the Chiericati Firmamento, Vicenza. Sixteenth century.

TAURUS

The standard image for Taurus is that of the bull, and there is fundamentally no difference between the first-century Roman image of Taurus in Figure 43 and that used in a modern zodiac in Berne (Fig. 44), or in the thirteenth-century Taurus from Chartres (Fig. 45) and the modern one from the marble fountain in the Signoria, Florence (Fig. 46). Some images portray the bull looking forwards, towards Aries, while others show it looking backwards towards the other zodiacal animals in its train. In some images, however, a convention has been developed in which only half a bull is shown – technically this is called the demi-Taurus – with the back half of the animal lost in clouds. This convention is partly derived from the constellation maps, some of which trace only half the bull in the pattern of stars (Fig. 47), but it is also a

43. Detail of a Roman Mithraic figure, of *c.* AD 50, from the Lapidary Museum at Arles. This realistic image of the bull of Taurus (so important in Mithraic imagery) is very little different from those used in modern astrological imagery.

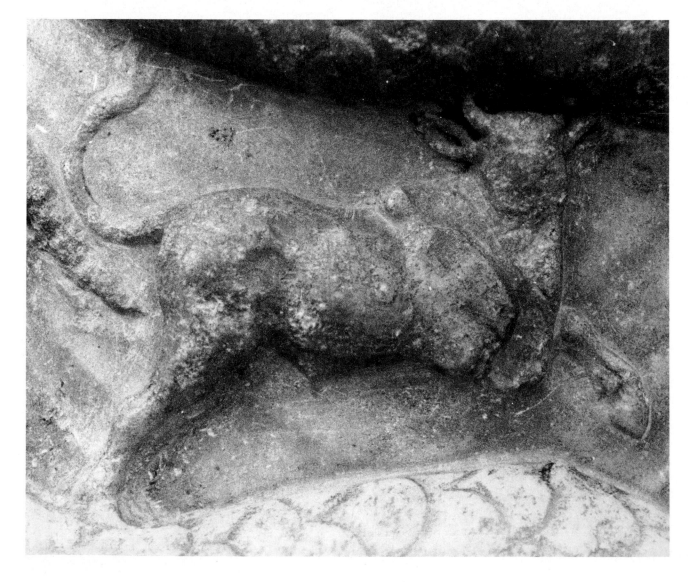

44. Detail of Taurus the Bull from a modern zodiacal doorway in the centre of Berne, Switzerland.

45. Taurus the bull, next to Leo the lion, on the archivolt of the north portal of the west front of Chartres Cathedral. Thirteenth century.

useful way of indicating the idea of the creature being a 'heavenly bull', reminding us that the earliest-known name for the sign (in Persian astrology) meant 'Bull of Light'. Perhaps this is what the designer of the Vezelay zodiac (Fig. 48) had in mind when he turned the back half of his bull into a fish, making the whole image a sort of composite mer-bull. This symbolism is rooted in magical imagery, however, in which the fish is used to indicate the spiritual realm. In such a mer-bull, therefore, we see the symbolist pointing to the extremely spiritualized nature of Taurus.

The modern sigil for Taurus (Fig. 49) is said by some to represent the horns and head of the bull, and it is this which Kircher illustrates in his own mythological zodiac (Fig. 35). However, some historians of symbolism trace in the sigil an attempt to

portray the larynx of the throat with the Eustachian tubes, which run from the larynx up to the ears. This explanation certainly fits the association which Taurus undoubtedly has with sound and music, while it also reflects the traditional rulership which the sign has been given over the human throat. This latter association explains why one so often finds a bull draped around the neck of the zodiacal man,

or leaping across the throat area (Fig. 50).

Some of the ancient Egyptian portrayals of Taurus show the creature with the solar disc on its back (Fig. 14), though, as the Denderah zodiac in Figure 34 indicates, this is not always the case. No doubt the solar disc is intended as a link with that other celestial bull, the sacred Apis. Athanasius Kircher has no hesitation in claiming that the bull of Taurus is a representation of the

46. Detail of marble zodiac in the fountain of the Piazza Signoria, Florence. The zodiac is modern, and divided into three parts – the one shown here represents the images (clockwise, from lower left) for Gemini, Taurus, Aries and Virgo.

47

Egyptian sacred bull, in whose form the god Osiris was believed to incarnate.

An interesting woodcut of *c*. 1527 (Fig. 51) shows Taurus in the form of a bull being wrestled to the ground by a man, while a maimed older man hobbles towards the animal as though intent on cutting its throat. In fact, the image is an allegory, relating to an opposition in the skies between Jupiter and Saturn, an opposition which occurs sufficiently rarely to frighten those who know little about astrology: many dire predictions were made about this particular 1527 opposition, but those who wrote the pamphlets which published the predictions failed to point out that the opposition occurs at least once every thirty years, and scarcely has an influence on

50 (right). The bull as ruler of the throat and speech in the medieval melothesic man. Early sixteenth-century woodcut.

51 (opposite). Astrological woodcut of 1527, from Lichtenberger's description of the effect of the opposition between Jupiter (in Taurus) and Saturn (in Scorpio).

52. Venus and her 'children' – the activities ruled by the planet, most of which are involved with luxurious enjoyment of the things of the body. From a sixteenth-century print.

social life of nations. The scorpion in the air relates to the maimed man, who is a personification of Saturn: the sickle in his hand is one of his standard attributes, a reminder that in early days Saturn was an agricultural god, though by the sixteenth century the sickle had become one of the destructive instruments of Saturn in his role of 'father Time'. It is the personification of Jupiter who is wrestling the Taurean bull to the ground – for reasons which are not clear, since the influence of Jupiter is generally regarded as being benign.

Taurus belongs to the Earth element – it is strong-willed, conservative, practical and sensuous, possessive and somewhat intractable. When its energies work creatively, then Taurus is often very productive in the realm of music, words and painting. No doubt this characteristic (perhaps otherwise unexpected in such an earthly sign) is due to the fact that the sign is ruled by the feminine planet Venus (Fig. 52). Without the softening touch of Venus, however, the sign tends to 'harden' and becomes unexpectedly violent, coarse, merely selfish and very fixed in attitude. It is this Venusless Taurus which 'El Haganah' had in mind when he coined the aphorism, 'Hast thou seen a man who argues with a wall? He is a fool; but he who argues with Sun in Taurus is even greater.'*

The section on San Miniato al Monte in Florence (p. 126) points out that Taurus is of great importance to this thirteenth-century marble zodiac, mainly because the year of the founding of the church and zodiac saw a remarkable gathering of no fewer than five planets in the constellation of Taurus. This explains why the arc of Taurus at San Miniato (Fig. 53) is directed towards the point of Sunrise over Florence, and why on the same Taurus—sunrise line, one finds a most interesting image of the Mithraic bull, another celestial bull, having its throat cut as part of the Mithraic sun-rituals (Fig. 54).

53. Image of Taurus from San Miniato al Monte in Florence. The arc of this sign is orientated towards that arc of the horizon which marks the daily position of sunrise over Florence. In 1207, when the San Miniato zodiac was laid down, there was a gathering of five planets in the constellation of Taurus.

54. Drawing of the bull being sacrificed by Mithras, from the fifteenth-century tomb of the Cardinal Prince of Portugal, in the basilica of San Miniato al Monte. Since the tomb was laid on the pathway which linked the arc of sunrise with Taurus, this Mithraic imagery was laid to commemorate the fact.

*From the 'Centiloquia of El Haganah', Astrology, Vol. 43, Dec. 1969. I am indebted to the editor of this important quarterly, Ronald C. Davison, for learning that 'El Haganah' was the pseudonym of C. E. O. Carter, the well-known writer on astrological subjects.

Zodiacal Horlogia

In Italy there are some impressive examples of large-scale calendrical systems designed in such a way that the passage of the Sun at midday throws a beam of light (through a specially fixed aperture) on to a specially calibrated chart. Almost certainly the largest of the Italian horlogia of this kind is that designed by the scientist Gassendi, in San Petronio, Bologna, but the most lovely is an external marble calendar, set in the arches beneath the Palazzo Publico, in the upper city, Bergamo, between the Duomo and the thirteenth-century octagonal baptistry (Fig. 55). The original was medieval, but the present marble design was cut and orientated in the eighteenth century (since when it has been restored several times). The Bergamo horlogium shows the daily positions of the Sun, traced in a calibrated marble, marked with the twelve zodiacal sigils (Figs. 56 and 57).

The most usual form of zodiacal horlogia, however, is in the form of a clock, the face of which displays the movement of the Sun (and sometimes the Moon) through the zodiacal signs.

55 (right). The horlogium at Bergamo, set in the pavement beneath the arches of the public buildings. In the distance is the octagonal baptistry, and to the left, the Corleoni chapel.

56 (above far right). Sigil for Cancer, sculpted in the calendrical calibrations of the horlogium at Bergamo.

57 (centre far right). Sigil for Gemini, sculpted in the calendrical calibrations of the horlogium at Bergamo.

The most lovely of these are in St. Mark's Square, Venice (Fig. 58), Modena, Padua (Fig. 59), and Berne, Switzerland (Fig. 60). All these were originally of the sixteenth century, but each has been restored several times in the intervening centuries: even so, in many cases, the original symbolism of the zodiacal images has been preserved. Probably the largest of the surviving zodiacal clocks is that inside the Cathedral at Strasbourg. The most impressive of modern zodiacal clocks is that above the main door of Bracken House, in Cannon Street, London (Fig. 61). The clock was installed in 1959, to the design of the engineers Thwaites and Reed. The face is about 2m (6.6ft) with three rotating rings and two small indicator windows. The outer ring revolves once an hour to indicate minutes; the middle ring marks the passage of hours, in a twelve-hour sequence, while the inner zodiacal ring

completes a circuit once a year, the pointer at the top indicating the position of the Sun within the sign for each day of the year. The design of the twelve images has been influenced by an Egyptian stylization – note, for example, the appearance of the dancing Twins of Gemini, or the stylized posture of Virgo. Capricorn is in the form of a goat (though in the Egyptian zodiac it was always a goat-fish), while the two fishes of Pisces leap around each other in a circular design: the traditional silver cord which usually binds the pair is missing. Like several of the medieval zodiacs, the Bracken House zodiac has a central Sun.

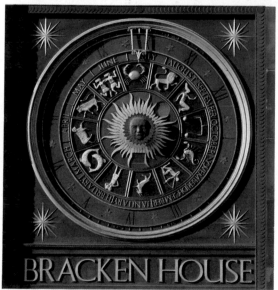

58 (far left top). The fifteenth-century zodiacal horlogium in St. Mark's Square, Venice.

59 (far left bottom). The fifteenth-century zodiacal horlogium in Padua.

60 (left). The sixteenth-century zodiacal horlogium in Bernc.

61 (bottom left). The modern zodiacal clock above the main door of Bracken House, in Cannon Street, London. The face of the central Sun bears a marked resemblance to Sir Winston Churchill, and it is said that this was intentional as the great statesman was a close friend of Lord Bracken, after whom the building is named.

62. Mercury, the ruler over Gemini and Virgo (both in roundels) – from a late fifteenth-century astrological text.

♊ GEMINI

The standard image for Gemini is that of the 'twins' – in classical times the twins Castor and Pollux – and in almost all images the emphasis is on the relationship between the two persons, a relationship which is ruled over by the dual Mercury (Fig. 62).

This is well in accord with the nature of the Geminian, which is concerned mainly with attempting to establish and maintain human relationship, through words and deeds. This 'need for contact', or 'need to relate' is expressed in a multitude of images

63. Gemini the twins, with the sigil for the sign, from Leopold of Austria's Astrorum Scientia *of 1489.*

64. The constellational roundel of Gemini the twins, from the thirteenth-century 'zodiacal arch' at Sacra di San Michele, Val di Susa.

65. Gemini the twins, from a Roman (second-century) Mithraic figure, in the Lapidary Museum, Arles.

which show the pair with arms around each other, as in the illustration from Leopold of Austria's *Astrorum Scientia* of 1489 (Fig. 63), kissing or cheek to cheek, as in the relief from Sacra di San Michele (Fig. 64), or at least holding hands. An early Roman example (Fig. 65) shows the pair of young men with their arms around each other in a friendly gesture. One medieval melothesic image (Fig. 19) entirely spurns the human figures, and reduces the image to a pair of clasping hands.

The modern symbol for Gemini (Fig. 66) is said to represent the idea of two people joining hands. The interesting Kircher mythological zodiac (Fig. 35) represents the

sigil in such a way, as a vestigial drawing of relationships. Some astrologers claim however that the symbol depicts two people I I standing on the same space of ground joined in the communication of ideas.

Gemini belongs to the Air element – it is versatile, idealistic, communicative, imitative, inventive, alert and inquisitive. The coarser grades tend to be superficial, restless, impatient and lacking in concentration.

The designers of zodiacs usually emphasize the idea of a conjoined couple, and normally attempt to represent the idea of their being in some sort of relationship. While the original twins were male – one of

66. Four medieval images of zodiacal signs, with corresponding sigils. The sigil for Gemini (top right) is the only one which has not changed in some small detail since the medieval period. That for Virgo (top left) is no longer merely a slanting stroke across the M, that for Pisces (bottom left) now has a horizontal tie-line (the 'silver cord' – see page 138), while that for Leo usually has a more substantial circle to the left.

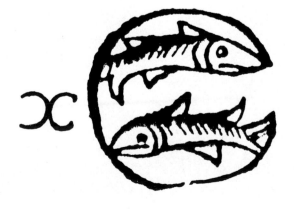

67. Personifications of the days of the week – Friday, Wednesday and Monday – from an English Shepherd's Calendar. The central image is of the planet Mercury, ruling over his two signs, Virgo and Gemini: the roundel below the money-bag shows the couple representing Gemini making love.

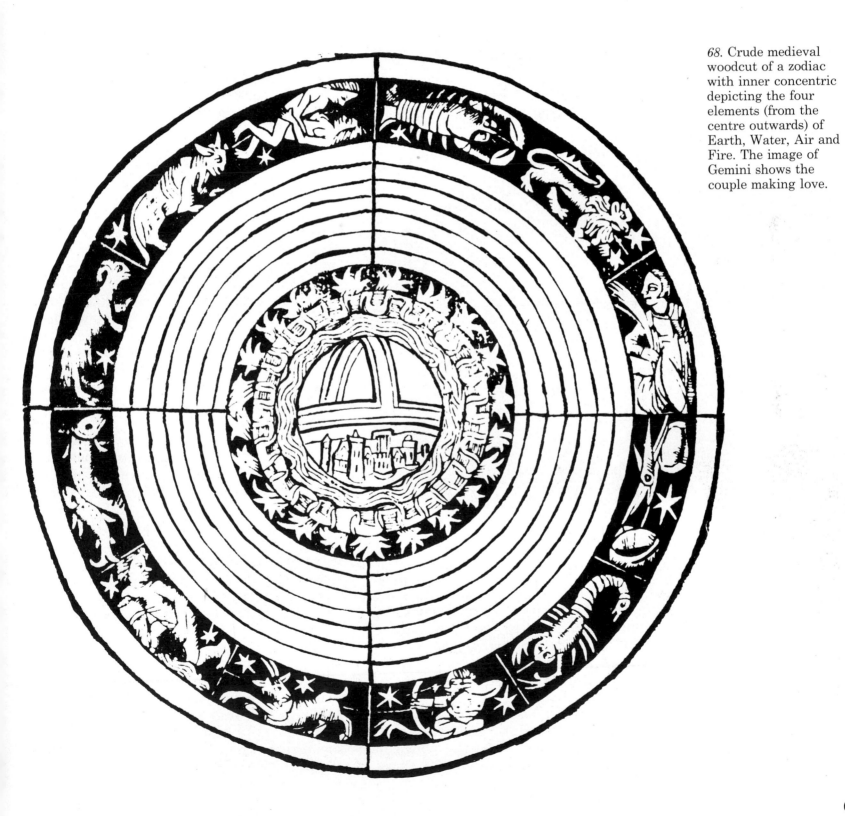

68. Crude medieval woodcut of a zodiac with inner concentric depicting the four elements (from the centre outwards) of Earth, Water, Air and Fire. The image of Gemini shows the couple making love.

69. Relief sculpture of Gemini from the thirteenth-century zodiac in the north porch of the west front of Amiens Cathedral.

tender images in zodiacal art, showing the couple gazing at each other, lightly holding hands, and clearly in love.

In early astrology great importance was attached to the idea that one of the twins was mortal, and the other immortal (Fig. 65), and this notion has survived in some of the medieval images. In Figure 32, for example, one of the twins is shown carrying a sickle, the emblem of mortality, while the other carries a musical instrument – probably a lyre, linking him with the higher realm, where the music of the spheres might be heard. This same notion is expressed even more graphically in the zodiacal man of Figure 70, for in a single image we find that the twin to the right of the figure holds a lyre, while the one to the left holds a sickle. The original imagery was involved with far more than the mere notion of twins – it reflected something of the basic nature of all human beings, who participate in the Earth, which is subject to decay and death, yet at the same time possess an immortal spirit. This explains why the early images insist on the pair having the same sex, and it was only when the real philosophical background to Gemini was forgotten, in the early medieval period, that the contrast between the 'material' and the 'spiritual' was lost, and the imagery descended into bawdy. The Roman twins were mortal and immortal – Castor and Pollux, respectively – but in later times these were generally ignored in favour of other famous or infamous twins, so that Athanasius Kircher, who knew very well the origin of the Roman symbolism, felt free to describe his pair of Geminians as representing Hercules and Apollo – a human hero and a god – a suggestion which explains the lyre (the attribute of Apollo) in some of the images.

them said to be mortal, and the other immortal in the Greek mythology – by the medieval period the notion of Gemini as a male–female pair had emerged, and, since the theme of relationship was the most important element within the symbol, it was not unusual for the cruder woodcuts, intended for the mass market, to portray Gemini as a couple making love, as for example in the tiny roundel which shows the rulership of Mercury over Gemini in Figure 67, and in Figure 68 from a late medieval French woodcut. In contrast with such bawdy, the Gemini on the portal of Amiens cathedral (Fig. 69) is one of the most

One amusing relic from the Gemini tradition is the engraving reproduced by the early nineteenth-century astrologer John Varley in his incompleted book on the facial characteristics of the twelve types, *A* *Treatise on Zodiacal Physiognomy*, the first part of which was published in 1828. Varley insisted that the ghost of a flea which the artist William Blake had drawn during a seance (Fig. 71) 'agrees in countenance

70. Gemini the twins with sickle and lyre, from a fifteenth-century translation of the Arabian Albumasar.

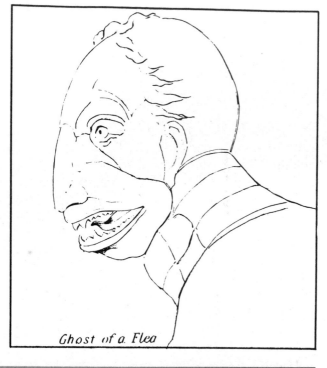

Ghost of a Flea

71. Engraving from Varley's *A Treatise on Zodiacal Physiognomy* of the ghost of a flea as seen and drawn originally by the artist William Blake. The image is said to incorporate the facial characteristics of the true Geminian.

with a certain class of persons born under Gemini'.

A charming modern image of Gemini, on the doorway of a block of flats in Berne (Fig. 72) has reverted to the ancient image of two children, one with his arms around the other – though in this case they are presented as sitting on the crescent Moon, which has no significant relationship with Gemini, yet which does evoke the idea of innocent childhood.

The most interesting image of Gemini which has made history is that in the woodcut published in 1665 by the English astrologer William Lilly (Fig. 73), which he claimed was a hieroglyphic relating to the future of England. The significance of the figure rested on the then well-known fact that London was ruled by Gemini, and the image of the twins hovering upside down over flames was taken as a prediction of a great fire. When the Great Fire of London did occur, in the following year, some people even went so far as to suggest that Lilly had started it in order to ensure that his prediction would come true.

72. Gemini the twins represented as an idyll of childhood, with the twins seated on a crescent moon (which, of course, has nothing to do with the sign itself). From a zodiacal door of a residential building in Berne.

73. Gemini hanging over a fire, from a 'hieroglyphic' drawn up by the seventeenth-century astrologer William Lilly, in 1665. This print was interpreted as a prediction of the Great Fire of London which broke out in the following year, destroying a greater part of the old city.

♋ CANCER

74. The crab as an image of Cancer, from the 1488 edition of Angelus' *Astrolabium Planum*.

The most frequently used image for zodiacal Cancer is that of the crab (Fig. 74), but in earlier forms of astrology the crayfish was often taken as the image for the sign, as may be seen from the fifteenth-century fresco at Padua (Fig. 75).

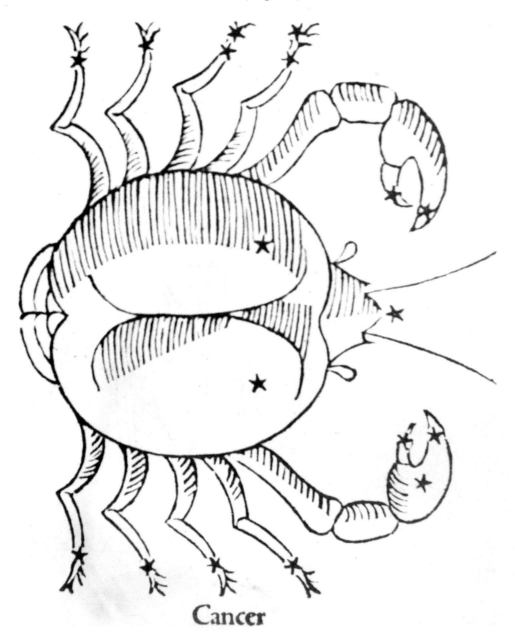

Cancer

The modern sigil for the sign (Fig. 76) is said by some to be a drawing of the female breasts, which are associated with the sign, and which are a useful reminder that Cancer is one of the nurturing signs, who takes pleasure in sustaining, feeding and generally protecting. At least one modern astrologer has argued that the symbol represents two spermatozoa, twisted together, intended to represent the male and female seed – for the sign Cancer is intimately linked with conception, and birth. Other astrologers see the sigils as drawings of an up-and-down movement, symbolic of the moodiness of the sign, while others say that the symbol is a vestigial drawing of the claws of the crab; one specialist suggests that the sigil is a drawing of two fixed stars – one casting its rays upwards, the other casting its rays downwards. The reason for this explanation lies in the peculiar nature of Cancer itself. Astrologers recognize that the sign Cancer has a greater proportion of powerful fixed stars within its arc than any other sign. Since fixed stars tend to 'lift up and throw down' those who are born under their influence, we find many eccentric people and geniuses born not only with their Sun or Ascendant in Cancer, but with fixed stars also prominent. In a recent survey, it was shown that the painter Salvador Dali was under the influence of the fixed star Propus, the Italian painter Modigliani had two powerful Cancerian fixed stars in his chart; the occultist H. P. Blavatsky had her Ascendant on the fixed star Castor; Einstein had his Ascendant on the fixed star Sirius, the French novelist Proust had his Sun on the fixed star Propus, while the psychologist Freud had his Ascendant with the fixed star Pollux.

75. The crayfish as an image of Cancer, from the fifteenth-century frescoes in the Salone, Padua.

76. Sigil for Cancer, from a hand-coloured *Astrorum Scientia* of Leopold of Austria, in the 1489 edition.

Cancer belongs to the Water element, and is by temperament romantic, shrewd, imaginative, sociable, domesticated, perhaps a little too passive, save in the realm of imagination. Under pressure, it may become very timid, self-absorbed and intensely moody.

Designers of zodiacs usually emphasize the 'shell' of the crab or crayfish, because this is part of the general association with the type 'born under Cancer'. In the zodiacal man (Fig. 32) Cancer has rule over the breast area, and over the rib-cage – it is, symbolically speaking, the shell which protects the heart, the seat of the emotions. This protective shell around the heart explains why the Cancerian is sometimes considered to be rather withdrawn, or self-engrossed: like the crab, the type is all armour on the outside, yet soft within. The modern zodiacs appear to have forgotten that Cancer was once considered a fresh-

water aquatic creature, for generally it appears now in the form of a crab – the magnificent modern zodiac on the façade of Bracken House, Cannon Street, in the City of London (Fig 61), is one example, while

78. Cancer the crab, gripping the first three letters of its own name between its claws, from the thirteenth-century marble zodiac in the Baptistry, Florence.

77 (far left). Zodiacal image of Cancer as a crab, from the stone doorway surround on the Sun Alliance Insurance building in Cheapside, London.

79. Cancer as a crab, in the quatrefoil of the zodiacal series in the north doorway of the west front of Amiens cathedral. Thirteenth century.

80. Cancer as a crayfish, from the west front of the cathedral of Notre Dame, Paris. Fourteenth century.

81. Cancer the crab, almost in the form of a scarabaeus beetle, among the thirteenth-century constellational roundels of the 'zodiacal arch' in Sacra di San Michele, Val di Susa.

another, only a few yards away, on the façade of the Sun Alliance Insurance building in Cheapside, is another (Fig. 77). The two enormous marble zodiacs in Florence – in San Miniato al Monte, and in the Baptistry – have Cancer in the form of crabs, though the latter does have all the appearance of a spider, hanging from the filigree web of the ornate zodiacal surrounds (Fig. 78). Probably the most beautiful example of the Cancer-crab in architecture is that on the portal of Amiens Cathedral, France (Fig. 79). The fact that the crab appears in the more important zodiacal imagery of medieval cathedrals might lead us to expect the same creature to be used in other church buildings of the period, yet this is not so, for we find on the west front of the medieval cathedral of Notre Dame, in Paris, a crayfish-Cancer (Fig. 80).

In the Egyptian demotic, the name 'Pagerhedj', the equivalent of our Cancer, is usually translated as 'scarabaeus', though in the Egyptian zodiac of Figure 14 the sign is not in the form of a scarabaeus beetle but is represented as a crab: oddly enough, the Cancer image of the Sacra di San Michele zodiac (Fig. 81) does suggest that it may have been derived from a manuscript tradition in touch with this view of the sign.

A Famous Zodiac – The Baptistry, Florence

Florence is a city which luxuriates in zodiacal lore, and there are three sets of complete zodiacal imagery in three public places – in the basilican church of San Miniato al Monte (Fig. 83), in the Baptistry opposite the cathedral in the centre of the old city (Fig. 82), and in the design of the fountain in the Piazza Signoria. The many museums display a vast amount of art involved with zodiacal lore, from astrological books, to medieval astronomical instruments, and magical zodiacal rings.

The Baptistry zodiac is set in the floor, off centre of the octagonal building, towards the cathedral. The zodiac is of the thirteenth century, and was probably constructed a little later

82. Florence at sunset: the city, ruled by zodiacal Aries, has three zodiacs in public buildings. These are in San Miniato al Monte, in the Baptistry opposite the Duomo (pictured here) and in the Piazza Signoria.

than the one in San Miniato, on the hill just outside the ancient walls of Florence (see p. 126). The Baptistry zodiac is now considerably worn and even defaced, yet most of the images can be discerned with ease (Figs. 78, 144 and 156) – but what is most important is that it is still possible to read the Latin inscription around the central sun of the zodiac (Fig. 84). This inscription is a palindrome – that is, a sentence designed to be read backwards and forwards, to give the same meaning. The Latin text reads:

ENGI ROTOR TE SOL CICLOS ET ROTOR IGNE

The text runs in a circle, and therefore has no real beginning or end (like the zodiac itself) yet it is clear that the Latin is inviting one to stand upon the image of the Sun, at the centre of the circle which represents cosmic space (the zodiac), and revolve with the Sun in its fiery cycle. There are 36 letters in the inscription, reminding us that in the medieval astrological system there were 36 decanates, with each of the twelve signs being divided into three. Thus, we are being invited not only to whirl through the twelve signs (as does the Sun), but also through the 36 decans, which, in the magical tradition, are linked with the planetary life of the zodiac.

In fact, when the human being stands on this central Sun, and visualizes himself whirling with the centre of the solar system, he actually becomes part of a vast machinery of symbolism, for he is identified both with the centre of the universe (which, in the medieval cosmology, is the Earth), with the Sun (a frequently used symbol for Christ), with the movement of the Sun (by which Time is measured), and with the fire or heat of the Sun (which in medieval symbolism is the love of Christ). The magical symbolism of this solar-centred zodiac becomes all the more remarkable when one recalls that it was believed that the Earth, and not the Sun, was the centre of the zodiacal band.

83 (left). The exterior of San Miniato al Monte, Florence. Built in 1207, this basilica contains one of the largest marble zodiacs in Europe.

84. The sun and its Latin inscription at the centre of the medieval zodiac in the Baptistry of St. John in Florence.

85. Leo the lion, ruled over by the personification of the Sun in the form of a king. From the fifteenth-century *De Sphaera* in the Bibliotheca Estense, Modena.

♌ LEO

The standard image for zodiacal Leo is a lion, and it has been represented in this form from the beginning of history – the earliest known names for the sign, derived from the Babylonian, call it 'the Great Light', and the sign is still ruled by the sun of our solar system (Fig. 85). Leo is therefore a lion, whether in the form of the somewhat kittenish lion of the Amiens zodiacal imagery (Fig. 86) or the severe-looking woodcut from Angelus' *Astrolabium Planum* of 1488 (Fig. 87).

The modern sigil for Leo (Fig. 88) is said to be a vestigial drawing of the lion's tail, and in his mythological zodiac, Athanasius Kircher lends all his considerable authority to this notion (Fig. 35). However, some modern astrologers are of the opinion that the symbol is a diagram of the emotional life of the Leonine. The small circle is taken as representing the heart, over which Leo is said to have rule, and the upward curve of the line is said to show the emotional uplift which the Leonine experiences when his

86. Leo the lion from the zodiacal series on the west front of Amiens cathedral.

87. Leo the lion among the constellations, from the 1488 edition of *Astrolabium Planum* by Angelus.

heart is taken by something of beauty or excitement in the world. Eventually, of course, the initial impetus of the emotions runs out, and the emotional response declines, which is why the curve is continued downwards. This upward search and downward decline explains on one level why the Leo type is constantly finding itself attracted to new projects, new excitements, but all too frequently finds itself unable to finish things as it would wish. Its search is for the 'completed', rather than for the completing.

Leo belongs to the Fire element, and the temperament of the sign is dignified, self-expressive, exuberant, flamboyant (indeed, often quite theatrical), hospitable and creative. In extreme cases the type may be selfish, arrogant, dogmatic and predatory. There is a sense in which all these

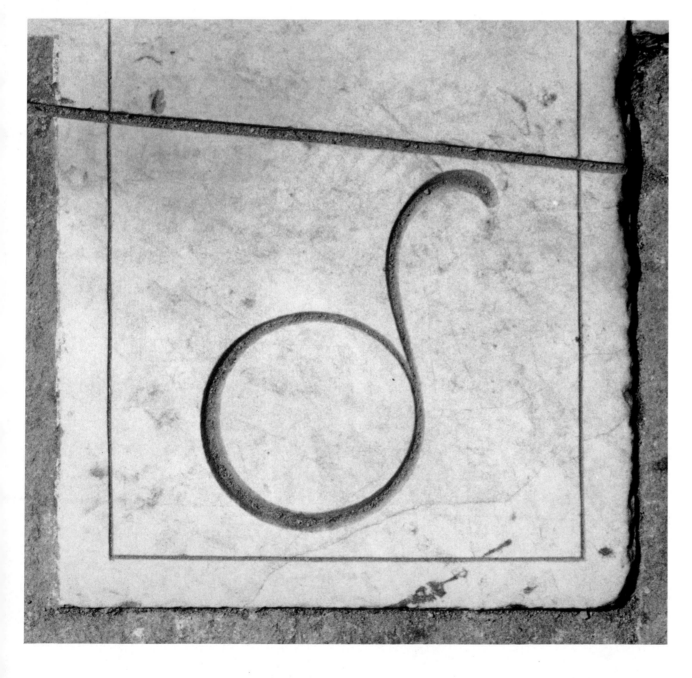

88. The modern sigil for Leo incised in the restored pavement calendar in the upper city, Bergamo. Usually, the sigil has a much smaller circle, and a more generous flourish.

89. Leo the lion climbing a tree, from among the zodiacal symbols on the façade of the cathedral of Notre Dame, Paris. Thirteenth century.

characteristics are associated with the traditional 'good' and 'bad' king – with the beneficient and tyrannical ruler. This is almost certainly why the standard image of Leo being ruled by the personification of the Sun (Fig. 85) often represents the two instruments of kingship which may be regarded as symbolizing the capability of good and bad – the sceptre and the sword. 'Leo', wrote El Haganah, 'loves the splendour of power; Uranus loves to exercise power; Capricorn is satisfied to possess it.'

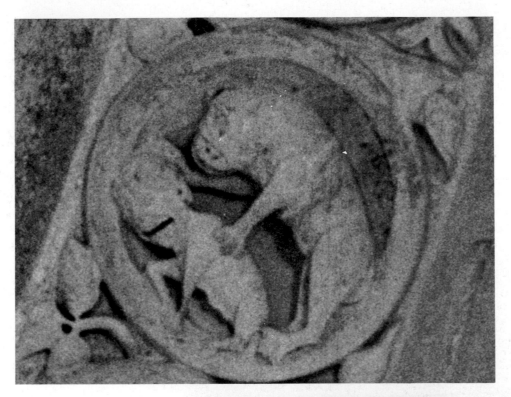

Designers of zodiacs usually attempt to express the dignity of Leo, or its more fearsome aspect (Figs. 89 and 90), as the classical 'king of the beasts' – a designation which expresses very well the Leonine attitude to itself as the natural leader or king of the domains which it surveys. The rigid formula of the lion has been broken very frequently by designers, however, and while the leonine form has always been preserved, some zodiacs vary the imagery in interesting or intriguing ways. For example, the Leo roundel in the Vezelay imagery (Fig. 91) shows an image which has been taken by some to represent the lion attacking a man. However, it is more likely that the designer had in mind the medieval fable (then believed to be zoologically true) that the lion cub was born shapeless, and was licked into shape by its mother: the recumbent figure may well be a badly

91 (above). Leo the lion involved in unconventional symbolism, from the register of zodiacal and labour symbols on the tympanum of the narthex of the Madeleine at Vezelay.

92 (right). Leo the lion was the origin of the symbol of the winged lion for the Evangelist St. Mark. This example is from the west front of Chartres cathedral.

93. The lion of St. Mark: from the nineteenth-century stained glass window in the parish church of Kilkhampton, Cornwall.

that rep
trology,
shows t
Moon (
and Ju

81

♍ VIRGO

94. The lic
the lecter
of San Mi
Monte, Fl
figure, wh
carved in
down the
church di
the marb
is an inte
the zodia
of the ch

The standard image for Virgo is a young woman holding a flower, a sheaf of corn, or some other relevant emblem, as for example on the face of the zodiacal clock from Venice (Fig. 96), but this is one of the signs where a great deal of variety in symbolism is permitted, mainly because the vision of womanhood has changed so much in the three thousand years that zodiacal images have been in use. The early medieval pictures of Virgo appear to derive their imagery from the fact that the Virgo of the heavens was often equated with the Virgin Mary – but we shall examine this trend in some detail at a later point. Such a religious influence explains, for example, the Virgo of Figure 97, which is from the 'zodiac' of Sacra di San Michele. The crude woodcut of Figure 98 is also of the 'Madonna' type, though the symbolism of the five-petalled flower is intended to point to the connection between the Queen of the Heaven and the magical symbol of the five-pointed star, generally called the pentagram, which

96 (opposite left). Image of Virgo – detail from the zodiacal horlogium in St. Mark's Square, Venice.

97 (opposite bottom right). Virgo the Virgin, holding what is probably intended to be an ear of corn, from among the constellational roundels on the so-called 'zodiacal arch' at Sacra di San Michele, Val di Susa. Thirteenth century.

98 (left). Virgo holding a flower, with five petals. Fifteenth-century woodcut.

in occult symbolism is linked with the secret elixir or Quintessence of the alchemists. A more modern image of Virgo, from the doorway of a block of flats in Berne, rejects all the religious symbolism, and presents her as a naked and voluptuous woman (Fig. 102). However, the prude Virgin and the voluptuous young woman are extremes between which a great variety of different feminine images have been evolved.

The modern symbol for Virgo (Fig. 99) is said by some to represent a vestigial drawing of the letters MV, Maria Virgo, in reference to the Virgin Mother of God. There are, however, many explanations for this curious sigil, the most interesting of which links it with the evolution of the symbols for Libra and Scorpio.

Virgo belongs to the Earth element, and the temperament is quiet, discriminative, shrewd, methodical, clever, graceful and intelligent. Under pressure it tends to become merely critical or carping – even shrewish.

The designers of zodiacs have generally attempted to illustrate the spiritual nature of the sign of Virgo – usually by deifying the image. The earliest known horoscopes of the Egyptians (Fig. 34) show Virgo as the equivalent of the goddess Isis, while even the Christian image-makers tended to link the zodiacal sign with their Virgin Maria. It is likely that the star which is found on the

99. Sigil for Virgo from the horlogium at Belgamo.

Gabriel visited Mary to announce that she was to be the mother of Jesus, she was spinning flax. The relationship between Mary and Christ is expressed astrologically in the fact that Virgo and Pisces are on opposite sides of the zodiac, and thus look constantly at each other in adoration (see, however, p. 143 for a survey of the connection between Pisces and Christ). Another strain of secret symbolism connected with Virgo is the late medieval attempt to link the imagery with the Grail symbolism, by substituting for the image of the virgin a holy chalice. Two excellent examples of this symbolism may be seen in the zodiac (top right, Fig. 103) and the zodiacal man (Fig. 19) from the sixteenth-century manuscript *The Guildbook of the Barber Surgeons of York*, now in the British Library.

100. The star on the shoulder of the Virgin Mary (a traditional symbol in all art prior to the 1600s) is derived from the star 'Spica' which figures in the constellational image of Virgo. Duccio's 'Virgin and Child', National Gallery, London.

101. Virgo from the thirteenth-century nave zodiac in San Miniato al Monte, Florence.

shoulder or maphorion of the Virgin Mary in thousands of medieval icons (Fig. 100) is derived from the image of the stellar Virgo. Within the constellation images there is a single powerful fixed star, called Spica ('ear of corn'), which, by symbolic extension, was adopted as the bread of life – Jesus the child of the Virgin Mary. This explains why some images of the Virgin Mary are linked directly with ears of corn, as in some early woodcuts in which the Virgin is studded with ears of corn, in a similar imagery to that of the stellar goddess, Virgo, who is studded with stars.

Another early-Christian throwback in the Virgo symbolism is the distaff, which is in the hand of several medieval images, as for example in the two zodiacs in Florence (Fig. 101). The distaff is essentially a reference to the Christian story that when

102 (right). Virgo as a sexually alert young woman, from a modern zodiac in the centre of Berne.

103 (opposite). Detail from a zodiac with a (rare) volvelle pointer, from *The Guildbook of the Barber Surgeons of York* in the British Library. The image for Virgo is that of a chalice – taken by some as a reference to the Grail legends.

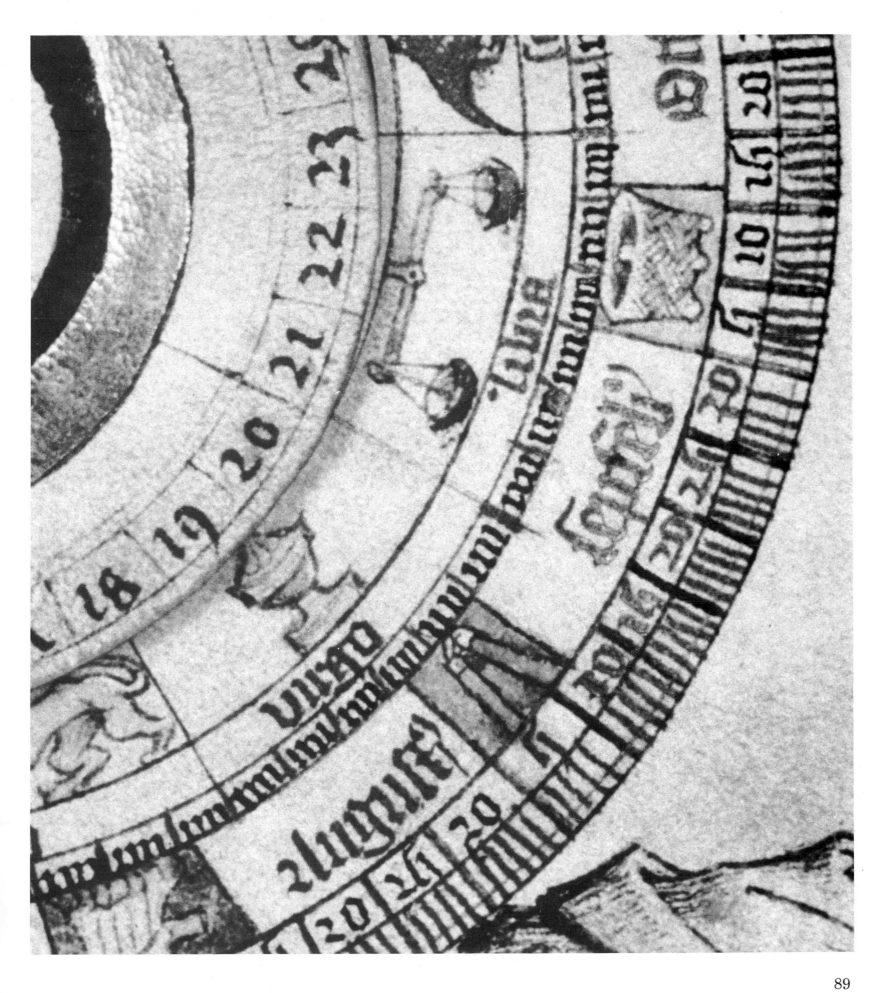

♎ LIBRA

The standard image for zodiacal Libra is a pair of scales (Fig. 106), though very often these are represented in the hands of a woman (Fig. 104). Designers of zodiacs usually emphasize the scales, as in the lovely Paduan fresco in Figure 106, but in some cases the female holding the balance is given an undue prominence, and the scales become so diminutive that they are almost lost, as happened in the San Miniato zodiac (Fig. 105). In the ancient Egyptian zodiac (Fig. 14), Libra is shown as a pair of scales, surmounted by a circle within which sits a god: the meaning of the Egyptian demotic word 'Ta-Akhet', the equivalent of our Libra, was 'place of sunrise', which might suggest that the encircled god is a solar deity. Almost certainly the poet Virgil would have known about this Egyptian god of Libra when, in his 1st Georgic, he

104. Image of Libra as a woman holding scales – from the zodiacal quatrefoils on the façade of the cathedral at Amiens. Thirteenth century.

addresses the Emperor Augustus (whose birthday saw the Sun just entering Libra), suggesting that this would be a fitting resting place for his soul, after death, when he would become a god himself.

In fact, Libra was an important sign for the Romans, as it was widely believed in ancient times that Italy itself was ruled by this sign, and that Rome itself was founded under the influence of Libra. According to the first-century Roman astrologer Tarrutius, Rome was founded in 754 BC, on 4 October. In modern times, however, it is generally agreed that Leo rules Italy and Rome. In spite of the Roman tradition, however, the coins struck in honour of Augustus usually emphasize the fact that at the time of his birth the Moon was on the cusp between Capricorn and Aquarius.

There is a tradition, preserved in several recondite hermetic books, that the zodiacal signs Scorpio and Libra were once a single figure, with the latter held in the claws of ♎ the scorpion. However, while such images do exist – as for example in the impressive zodiacal imagery in Sacra di San Michele (Fig. 107) and a few woodcuts of the late fifteenth century (Fig. 108) – the earliest zodiacs do show them as separate signs. It is likely that at one time the constellational imagery did portray the two as a single figure, and in some cases Libra was even referred to as 'chelae', or 'claws of the scorpion', and it is equally true that the constellational imagery has at times been confused with the signs of the zodiac, but the truth is that for all intents and purposes Libra has been regarded as a sign in its own right since the earliest recorded history of the zodiac. It is indeed the fact that the scorpion grasps the scales, in Figure 107, which is one of the indicators that the Sacra

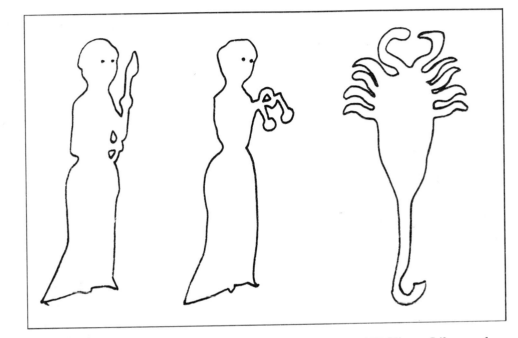

di San Michele imagery belongs to the constellational tradition, rather than to the tropical zodiac of signs.

The sigil for Libra (Fig. 109) is usually claimed to be a drawing of a pair of scales. However, the Egyptian hieroglyphic for the sign shows an image of the sunset over the ⚖ Earth and it is clear that this image, rather than 'scales', is the origin for the sigil. The relevance of this Egyptian hieroglyphic is that it represents the male (the Sun image) and female (the horizontal Earth) in a sort of balance, each in their rightful places, yet with a space of air between them: the domain of Libra is this 'space of air', in which it can act as a mediator between the male and the female, and introduce relationships between the spiritual (the Sun) and material (the Earth) aspects of the world. In the standard horoscope figure, the place of Libra marks the symbolic point of sunset (the Descendant point), and it is obvious that this Egyptian symbol, which

105. Virgo, Libra and Scorpio. Drawings from the images in the San Miniato zodiac of 1207. Note the small size of the balance held in the hands of the Libra woman.

91

106. Image of Libra as a pair of scales, from the sixteenth-century frescoes in the Salone, Padua.

107. Libra in the claws of Scorpius – from the thirteenth-century 'zodiac-arch' in Sacra di San Michele, Val di Susa.

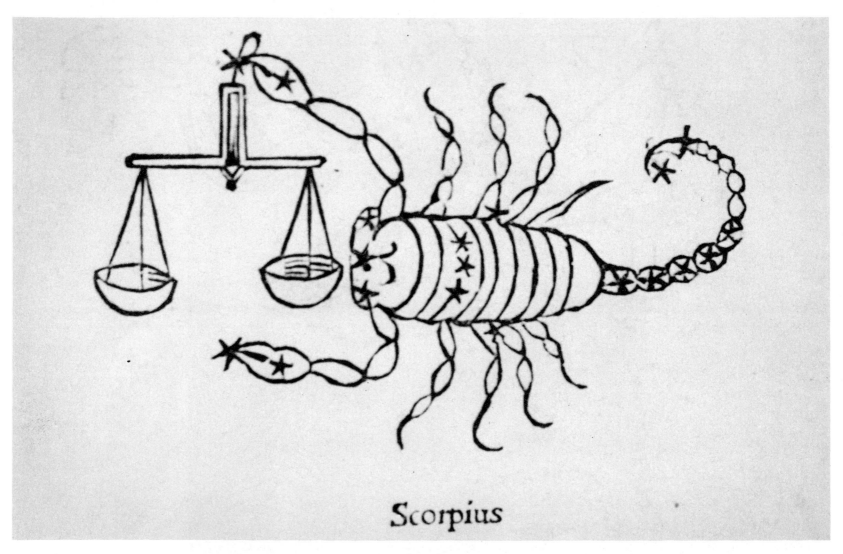

Scorpius

108. Libra in the claws of Scorpius – constellation illustration from Angelus' *Astrologium Planum* of 1488.

reveals the inner space where reconciliation and harmonization may take place, is a more fitting origin for the sign than a primitive pair of scales, even though the idea of 'balance' is so important a part of the Libran psychological make-up. The horoscope cast for Jesus Christ by the astrologer Ebenezer Sibly gives a Libran ascendant – no doubt because Christ is the archetypal harmonizer.

Libra belongs to the Air element, its temperament being gentle, sensitive, peaceful, delicate, affectionate, perceptive, elegant, orderly and changeable. In excess, when the type loses its sense of balance, the impractical side becomes emphasized, and there may be a tendency for the Libran to indulge in passivity or even downright laziness. All the associations of the gentle ruler Venus are directly linked with Libra – the 'children of Venus' generally giving themselves over to self-indulgence in physical and spiritual appetites (Fig. 52).

94

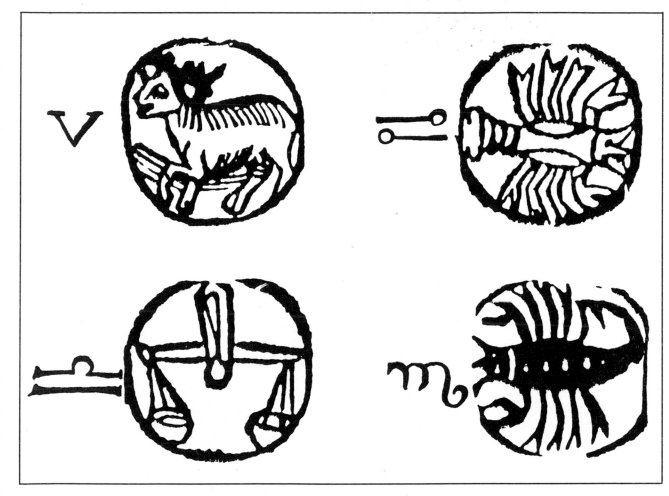

Some early Roman literature claims that Libra was first added to the Roman zodiac, and, even though this is not true, the notion of Libra being created as the twelfth sign to complement an eleven-sign zodiac has entered into poetic fancy. Milton visualizes God as creating Libra (the 'golden scales'), to draw a line between the good and rebellious angels:

Th' Eternal, to prevent such horrid fray,
Hung forth in heav'n his golden scales, yet seen
Between Astraea and the Scorpion sign;

These short lines remind us that 'Astraea' is one of the poetic names for the constellation Virgo. While the Romans certainly did not 'invent' or introduce Libra to the zodiac, it is true to say that they gave us the word itself, even if this was based on a misunderstanding. Long before the Romans, the Greeks had called the sign and constellation by several words, one of which translates as 'weight': it seems that the old Sicilian-Greek equivalent word was 'Libra', from whence the Romans took the word we now use, but changed its meaning from 'weight' to 'scales'.

A Famous Zodiac – Sacra di San Michele

110. Exterior of the monastery of Sacra di San Michele, in the Val di Susa, which houses the most ancient constellational carvings of the post-classical period.

111. The top arch of the so-called 'Staircase of the Dead' in Sacra di San Michele, Val di Susa. The constellational images are in the shadows behind the façade.

The oldest programme of zodiacal symbolism in Europe is probably that found in the fortress-like monastery of Sacra di San Michele in the Val di Susa (Fig. 110). The zodiacal images are carved on the doorway at the top of what is now ominously called 'The Staircase of the Dead' (Fig. 111), but there is some evidence to suggest that the entire doorway was not originally part of the main fabric of the monastery, but was moved, lock stock and barrel, from the octagonal baptistry which formerly stood some distance from the monastery, traces of which may still be seen.

The zodiacal imagery in the Sacra is early twelfth century, and consists of a number of zodiacal motifs which are located vertically on the columns of the doorway. The twelve images are contained in roundels, and are named, but two of the images (Scorpio and Libra – Fig. 107) are merged, with the result that the images are represented in only eleven roundels. In fact, to be quite precise, the images appear to relate to the zodiacal constellations, rather than to the signs, for Scorpio is presented as Scorpius, and is merged with Libra (see p. 91), as sometimes happens in the constellational images.

Of particular interest among the images is that for Gemini (Fig. 64), which portrays two men embracing (the heavenly twins, derived from the classical mythology, which makes one mortal, the other immortal), and the distinctive Capricorn, which is in the form of a winged dragon-bodied goat.

The sequence of the images does not follow the normal circular pattern. At the top is Aquarius followed by Pisces (Fig. 112), leading into the normal sequence commencing with Aries. The first six images are 'read' vertically, while the remainder are read from the side. The curious arrangement is almost certainly intended to reflect the sequence of planetary rulerships which was transmitted to Europe from Roman times by way of the Arabs. Thus, Aquarius and Capricorn (top and bottom) are both ruled by the outer planet Saturn; while Pisces and Sagittarius (second and eleventh) are ruled by Jupiter. Aries and Scorpio (third and tenth places) are ruled by Mars; Taurus and Libra (fourth and ninth) are ruled by Venus; Gemini and Virgo (fifth and eighth) are ruled by Mercury; and the Moon and Sun rule the two central signs Cancer and Leo, respectively. The sequence may be summarized, using the spelling on the actual column itself:

AQUARIUS	Saturn	CHAPRICORNUS
PISCES	Jupiter	SAGITTARIUS
ARIES	Mars	SCORPIUS
TAURUS	Venus	LIBRA
GEMINI	Mercury	VIRGO
CANCER	Moon Sun	LEO

112 (far left). Pisces roundel from the constellational series in Sacra di San Michele.

113 (left). Centaurus and the 'Bestia' – detail from the constellational series in Sacra di San Michele, Italy.

Of course, modern astrology has a different set of planetary rulerships, designed to accommodate the newly discovered planets, such as Neptune, Uranus and Pluto, but the sequence above is found in the most important textbooks dealing with the zodiac known to the medieval astrologer.

On the further side of the arch, also depicted on the vertical column, but this time in floral-edged squares, is an exciting collection of eighteen constellations, which are (like the zodiacal sequence) named in Latin. In descending order, the names read:

(AQUILA), DELFINUS, PEGASUS, DELTOTON, ORION, LEPUS, CANIS, ANTICANIS, PISTRIX, ERIDANUS, CENTAURUS, CETUS, NOTHIUS, ARA, HYDRA.

Alongside Hydra are the unnamed images for Corvus and Amphora, and in the hand of the Centaur is the image of a further constellation formerly named 'Bestia', but in later constellation maps called 'Wolf'. In this imagery, however, the Bestia looks rather like a hare, or rabbit (Fig. 113). The Latin name 'Nothius' is the equivalent of the Southern Fish, while Pistrix is the Roman equivalent of the modern Cetus, or Whale. There is some confusion in this image (Fig. 114), however, and it is likely that the artist, unfamiliar with the astrological symbolism, made a mistake in presenting here an image of the ship of Argo.

The Sacra zodiacal imagery is older than the San Miniato zodiac (see p. 126) by almost a century. The complex symbolism of the San Miniato zodiac, which uses zodiacal imagery with stellar and solar lore on an incredible level of symbolism, demonstrates a complete confidence in the ability of artists to use the newly inherited pagan lore for Christian purposes. In comparison, the symbolism of the Sacra zodiac appears insubstantial. The difference in a century between the two sets of zodiacal images indicates the extent to which artists and theologians of that period assimilated zodiacal lore, and almost eagerly began to turn pagan lore into a symbolic programme which could be used in places of Christian worship.

If the San Miniato zodiac represents the complete confidence in this mastering of the pagan lore, the zodiacal imagery at Sacra points to the uncertainty experienced by artists and theologians at the new learning, which was still tinged with the 'heresies' of the Arabians. There is something almost innocent in the way in which the imagery for constellation Ara (Altar) ignores the pagan lore, which has the altar as a receptacle for a flame, and turns it into a simple Christian altar, almost with a visible altar cloth (Fig. 115), and turns the Southern Fish (Nothius) into the theological image of Christ, the Eucharistic sacrificial fish, above the altar.

114 (top). Cetus, the constellational image from the series in Sacra di San Michele, Italy.

115 (above). Ara, the ancient constellation of the 'Altar', which is normally represented as a pagan altar, in the constellational series in Sacra di San Michele. In this series it has been turned into a Christian altar.

♏ SCORPIO

The standard image for Scorpio is that of a scorpion (Fig. 116), but the artistic interpretation of what a scorpion actually looks like has been very free, with the result that we have zodiacal images which look almost like camels, as in the Vezelay zodiac (Fig. 117) or a carapacious monster as in Figure 118, on the façade of Amiens cathedral. The most biologically accurate drawings and sculptures tend to come from the Mediterranean zodiacs, from regions where there is no doubt whatsoever what scorpions look like – a good example is the surviving antique constellational map of Figure 17, but the scorpion among the zodiacal images on the façade of the Bank of Scotland, in Edinburgh, is also very convincing (Fig. 120).

The modern sigil for Scorpio is said by some to represent the male sexual parts, over which the sign has rule in the image of the zodiacal man (Fig. 19). However, the occultists claim a much more sophisticated origin for the sign, suggesting that the sigil is a vestigial drawing of the severed tail of a serpent. Yet the many medieval sigils for

116. Image of Scorpio from the nineteenth-century series used by 'Libra' in *Astrology – its Technics and Ethics*.

117. Image of Scorpius from the roundels on the tympanum of the narthex in the Madelaine, at Vezelay. The designer had clearly not looked at scorpions.

118. Image of Scorpio
from the zodiacal
quatrafoils on the
façade of Amiens
cathedral.

100

119. The Scorpionic eagle of St. John is in the top right roundel. In clockwise direction starting from the Eagle there is the Taurean bull of St. Luke, the Leo of St. Mark, and the Aquarian winged human of St. Matthew. Nineteenth-century, decorative detail on the pulpit in Harkstead church, Suffolk.

120. Nineteenth-century image of Scorpio on the façade of the Bank of Scotland in George Street, Edinburgh.

Scorpio were quite different from the modern one, as the example in Figure 121 demonstrates, and so it is difficult to justify this most interesting theory. However, the earliest known symbol is the Egyptian demotic, which does represent Scorpio as an erect serpent. In some circles, it is commonplace for astrologers to provide two symbols for Scorpio – the standard scorpion and a vestigial drawing of an eagle, for reasons which are set out below.

Just as it is necessary to distinguish between Scorpius and Scorpio (that is, between the constellational image and the tropical zodiac), so astrologers often distinguish between the 'degenerate Scorpio' and the 'regenerated Scorpio', perhaps on the grounds that the sign which rules the sexual parts of man might be used for destruction or for preserving and continuing the life forces, depending upon the attitudes of the person concerned. In some forms of astrology a distinction is made between the symbols used to denote these two different Scorpios – the degenerate form is represented by the earthbound scorpion, while the life-enhancing Scorpio is represented by the heavenly-aspiring eagle. It is not surprising that when the early Christians adopted zodiacal lore to symbolize their four evangelists, and chose Scorpio for the intense St. John, they should choose the form of the eagle rather than the scorpion: this explains why the

121. Seventeenth-century manuscript recording the sigils used for the signs of the zodiac, in the Public Library, Lucca. Note the curious form for Scorpio, which fell into desuetude in the following century.

122 (right). The planet Mars, ruler over the signs Aries and Scorpio. The 'positive' rule was over the Ram, while the 'negative' rule was over the Scorpion: however, these terminologies are rarely used in modern astrology, and Scorpio is now thought to be ruled by the planet appropriately named after the ancient God of the Underworld, Pluto. From the fifteenth-century *De Sphaera* in the Bibliotheca Estense, Modena.

123 (opposite). Sting of Scorpio with knots in it. The curious design is almost certainly influenced by the line of stars which are generally seen as being representative of the curve of the stellar scorpion, and which were sometimes represented in crude woodcuts.

Il bellicoso marte sempre infiama
Li animi alteri al guerreggiare et sforza
Hor questo hor quello ne saria sua brama

104

thousands of sets of Evangelist images (Fig. 119) represent the Scorpionic St. John in the image of an eagle.

For all its Earth or Air symbolic undertones, Scorpio belongs to the Water element, and its deep, passionate nature is often explained in terms of the water being contained within a deep well – such water serves the community, and is a source of life, yet it may easily be poisoned, and, when polluted, spread diseases. So it is with the Scorpionic temperament, which in the regenerative scale is penetrating, inspirational, extremist, magnetic, intense, creative, shrewd, self-confident, masterful and healing. In contrast, the degenerative Scorpionic is often given to anti-social behaviour, and to criminal activities, being a law unto himself: such a direction brings a sense of violence and intrigue, rebelliousness, cruelty, self-indulgence, and the like. The modern planetary rulership of Pluto, the ancient god of the underworld, points to both the hidden depths within the sign, and to the ease with which the earthbound energies at the centre of the Earth (Pluto's domain) may explode outwards in fury. Before the discovery of Pluto in our solar system, the sign was ruled by 'negative Mars', the planetary god who is so often linked with violence, as the nominal 'God of War' (Fig. 122). However, we should remember that soldiers are rarely the cause of war – they merely attempt to solve problems created by politicians, or despots, and the keynote of soldiering is obedience and courage. The disciplined Scorpio is a most powerful individual, prepared to wield the scalpel of healing with more willingness than he will touch the sword of Mars.

Designers of zodiacs attempt to illustrate the somewhat fearsome nature of the

124. The image of Scorpio in the north doorway of the west front of Chartres cathedral. Thirteenth century.

Scorpio, if only to illustrate the power within the sign: more often than not, this characteristic is expressed by the representation of a fearsome tail, with its sting, which reminds us that in the Babylonian zodiac Scorpio was called 'the Stinger'. Some of the stings have cruel nippers on the ends, while others are snake-like, and yet others are knotted and ominous (Fig. 123). This 'knotted tail' is almost certainly derived from an interpretation of the line of stars which make up the tail of the stellar

Scorpius, and which have sometimes been used to represent the entire constellation (Fig. 126). The scorpion on the façade of Chartres cathedral (Fig. 124) is quite evil-looking, as is the scorpion with the balance of Libra in its claws from Sacra di San Michele (Fig. 107). However, the scorpion on the façade of Notre Dame, Paris, has been reduced to a cypher which would evade identification, were it not evident from the sequence that Scorpio is intended (Fig. 125). One consequence of Scorpius (to give the constellation its proper name) being intimately associated with Libra is that in some modern zodiacal images Scorpio is given a size quite out of proportion to its position in the constellations or zodiac. A medieval example of this may be seen on the clock-face imagery of the zodiacal horlogia in Padua (Fig. 127) for the image of the scorpion is extended over two signs, between Sagittarius and Virgo, with Libra, the proper tenant of the sign after Virgo, reduced to a mere cypher by the sting of the creature, rather than in its claws.

125. The curious Scorpio on the west front of the cathedral of Notre Dame, Paris. Thirteenth century.

126 (overleaf left). Fanciful depiction of the constellation images in an early sixteenth-century textbook: the images portrayed have little or no relationship to the actual patterns of even the most important stars in the skies.

127 (overleaf right). Detail of the zodiacal clock in the Piazza dei Signori, Padua. The detail shows Virgo, Scorpio, Sagittarius and Capricorn (in the form of a goat). Note that Scorpio spreads itself over two full arcs of the zodiac, thereby displacing Libra: this is certainly a throwback to the constellational imagery.

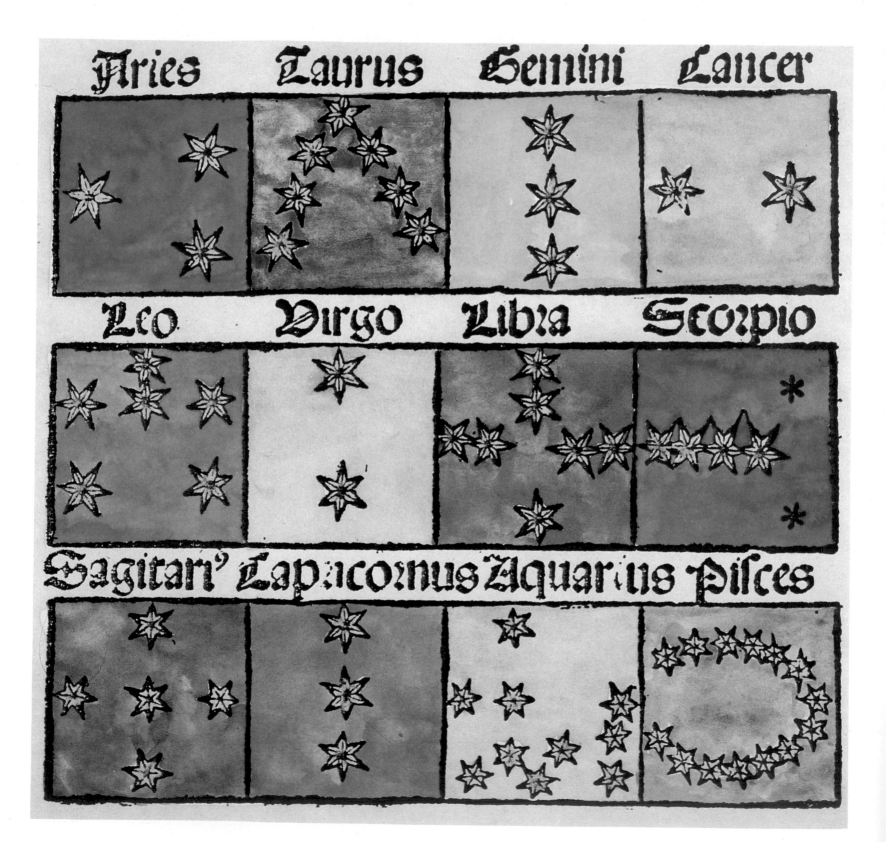

108

SAGITTARIUS

128 (right). Image of Sagittarius as a centaur-bowman. From a late fifteenth-century edition of the astrological writings of Albumasar.

129 (opposite bottom). Image of Sagittarius as a Pan-bodied bowman, from the north porch of the west-front of Amiens cathedral. Thirteenth century.

130 (opposite right). Thirteenth-century constellational manuscript showing Sagittarius as a Pan-bodied bowman. British Library, London.

The standard image for Sagittarius in modern times is the bowman, as represented in one of the zodiacal roundels of the ruling planet Jupiter (in Fig. 131), but in early astrology the sign was almost always represented as a centaur drawing a bow – in other words, as a half-man, half-animal (Fig. 128). This was not without its symbolic force, since the nature of the sign is such that the personality is exceedingly human, yet is often weighed down by the appetitive life of the body, even by a powerful love for the good things of life which sometimes impedes his or her own development.

The modern symbol for Sagittarius is said to be a vestigial drawing of the bow and arrow carried by the animal-man in the image. However, some esotericists claim that the symbol may only be properly understood if it is seen as an arrow lifting up a cross. In this symbolism, the arrow is that of spiritual aspiration, reaching skywards into the spiritual realm, while the cross represents the four elements, the materiality of the physical world, which the Sagittarian has to carry. This notion of 'lifting materiality into the spiritual' is a very important aspect of the Sagittarian nature, and explains why the sign is linked with education, teaching, lecturing, writing and so on – those arts and professions by which mankind is civilized.

Sagittarius belongs to the Fire element, and its nature is open, honest, dignified, optimistic, loyal, independent and generous. In excess the type tends to be prodigal to a point of fault, self-indulgent, conceited and dogmatic – it is as though such a person has regressed into the lower nature, and has become forgetful of his spiritual origins.

Designers of zodiacs are usually keen to express the duality of the Sagittarian

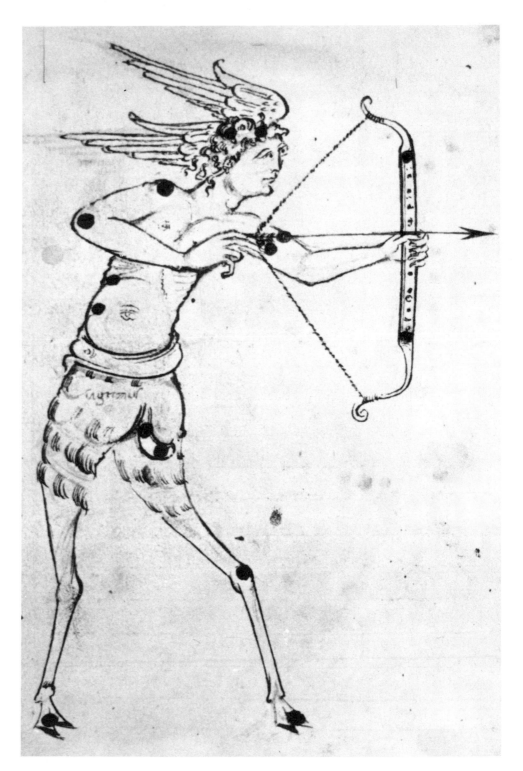

131. The planet Jupiter, with the roundels of the two signs over which he has rule: Sagittarius and Pisces. In this medieval image Sagittarius is represented in the form of a bowman.

132. Medieval constellational image of Sagittarius, the centaur-bowman. Fourteenth century. British Library, London.

133 (right). Image of a wild-haired centaur-like Sagittarius, from among the zodiacal roundels in the tympanum of the narthex of the Madeleine, Vezelay.

134 (below). Thirteenth-century marble carving of Sagittarius from the so-called 'zodiacal arch' in Sacra di San Michele, Val di Susa.

135 (opposite). Capricorn and Sagittarius from a modern zodiac on the façade of the hotel Lo Zodiaco, in Sirmione, Italy.

nature – the half which aspires towards spiritual perfection, towards civilization, and the bestial, or animal-like, half, which seeks carnal enjoyments. Usually it is sufficient to show half the body in human form, and for the symbol of the upward-directed arrow to reveal its own rather obvious symbolism, but designers often attempt to emphasize the lower nature of the Sagittarian in original forms. The Sagittarius image at Amiens (Fig. 129) is especially interesting, for the lower part is not that of a horse (as in the centaur imagery) but that of a goat, reminding one of the pictures of the Roman god of nature, Pan. The arrow is being aimed downwards, rather than towards the skies, but this is still in accordance with Sagittarian symbolism since this figure is placed next to the entrance to the cathedral, with the arrow pointing towards the door, giving the symbolic impression that the archer is still aiming into spirituality – in this case, into the spiritual realm which belongs to Christ. Fewer images of Sagittarius express more powefully the duality of its nature than these Pan-Christian ones. This Pan image is not unique to Amiens, by any means, and a fine example from the medieval manuscript tradition is found in a thirteenth-century constellational text from the British Library (Fig. 130), where the pronounced sexual part of the figure is a sly reference to the reputation which the Sagittarian has for enjoyment of sex. It will come as no surprise to learn that the earliest reference in classical literature to the sign actually names it as a Satyr. The Egyptian zodiac from Denderah (Fig. 34) shows the image in centaur-form, though with the mane of a lion. Another quirk of zodiac design is that Sagittarius is often represented as looking backwards, and firing the arrow over his own back, as may be seen in the example manuscript illumination from the British Library (Fig. 132) and in the roundels in Vezelay (Fig. 133), in Sacra di San Michele (Fig. 134) and in a modern zodiac from Sirmione (Fig. 135).

The spiritual side of Sagittarius is often emphasized, to the detriment of the lower nature – this is especially so in the modern zodiacs, for the inner symbolism of the centaur has largely been forgotten. The dramatic, entirely human archer in Figure 136, from a modern zodiac in Berne, is typical of this approach: the six-pointed star upon the bow reminds us of the spiritual aspiration of the types, yet it is as though the lower bestial nature has been ignored.

This is not so in the medieval woodcut (Fig. 128), for the lively step of the horse-body shows the powerful energies of the lower nature to great advantage, while the

spiritual aspiration is expressed in the fact that the arrow is tipped with a star, rather than with the usual dart. In fact, the attempts to trace in the pattern of the constellations assigned to Sagittarius almost always use the powerful yellow star, the gamma of the constellation, to mark the tip of the arrow, as we may see from the Arabian image in Figure 137, which shows both the dart and the circle which represents the important star, called by the Arabians, 'Al Nasl' (the Point). The arrow is of great importance to the Sagittarian symbolism, not merely because it is linked with the stars (symbols of the archetypes, of the aspiring spirit), but because in ancient Roman times the sign was not always called Sagittarius but Sagittifer ('arrow-carrier'). Yet some of the old names for the sign reflect the duality more than the word Sagittarius – it was 'Semivir', or Halfman and even Minotaurus, even though it did not have the head of a bull, like the classical minotaur.

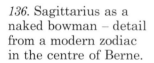

136. Sagittarius as a naked bowman – detail from a modern zodiac in the centre of Berne.

137. The constellation of Sagittarius, from an eighteenth-century Arabic manuscript.

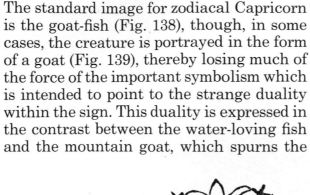

♑ CAPRICORN

The standard image for zodiacal Capricorn is the goat-fish (Fig. 138), though, in some cases, the creature is portrayed in the form of a goat (Fig. 139), thereby losing much of the force of the important symbolism which is intended to point to the strange duality within the sign. This duality is expressed in the contrast between the water-loving fish and the mountain goat, which spurns the water, and seeks to climb upwards to the clouds. The symbolism is related to the fact that in magical lore water represents the unconscious, or psychic powers, while the striving up a mountain represents the intellectual consciousness. The true Capricornian is often consciously intent on climbing the mountain – be it a career or a life-ambition – and by so doing, standing aloof from the crowd. The unconscious fear of the Capricornian is that he may slip back down the mountain, and merge with the waters, where his or her own consciousness may be lost.

The symbol for Capricorn is said by some to be a vestigial drawing of the horns of the goat. However, the sigil has many variant forms, as for example in the sigil marking the extreme point of the sun at the Winter Solstice on the Bergamo zodiac (Fig. 140), or among the twelve sigils presented by the magician Agrippa in his book of 1530, *De Occulta Philosophia* (Fig. 24). The rationale behind the first of these symbols is that it represents the same duality which we traced between the fish and the mountain goat (namely, conscious versus subconscious forces) – the V of the symbol represents the conscious aspirations, the straight lines representing the cutting aspect of the conscious mind, which seeks always to define, and tie down with words and concepts. The curvilinear form, on the other hand, represents the fluidity of the water, where the fish is at home – the symbol of the unconscious, of that which seeks to understand in terms of lateral thinking. In some rare cases, the curvilinear fish-form is reduced to being almost an afterthought – as for example in the interesting drawing of the fish-tailed goat in the melothesic man in Figure 141.

138. Capricorn as a goat-fish, from an Italian woodcut of *c.* 1520.

139. Capricorn as a goat – in the zodiacal segment to the extreme left.

Capricorn belongs to the Earth element, and the conscious life is industrious, cautious, methodical, ambitious, dependable, efficient, honest, systematic and undemonstrative. When under pressure, the type becomes secretive, miserly, fearful, rigid, suspicious and egotistical.

The designers of zodiacs usually attempt to represent the duality of the goat-fish in some meaningful way, and there are a large number of representations of the Capricornian goat-fish which play with the unlikely combination with surprising variety. The Amiens zodiac portrays a two-legged goat with a tail which is almost serpentine, rather than fish-like, while the esoteric zodiac of the *Book of Hours* of the Duke of Berri (Fig. 142) represents Capricorn as a goat with a shell body – perhaps a throwback to the secret symbolism which interested Hieronymus Bosch. The zodiacal roundel of what is called 'Chapricornus' in the Val di Susa zodiac (Fig. 143) portrays the creature with wings: this also is two-

140 (right). Sigil for Capricorn, signifying the point of the winter solstice, in the medieval pavement calendar in the upper city at Bergamo.

141 (opposite left). Capricorn the goat, with a fish-tail. After an Italian melothesic figure of the early sixteenth century.

142 (opposite right). Melothesic figure from the *Book of Hours* of the Duke of Berri. Note that Capricorn has lost its tail, but gained a shell.

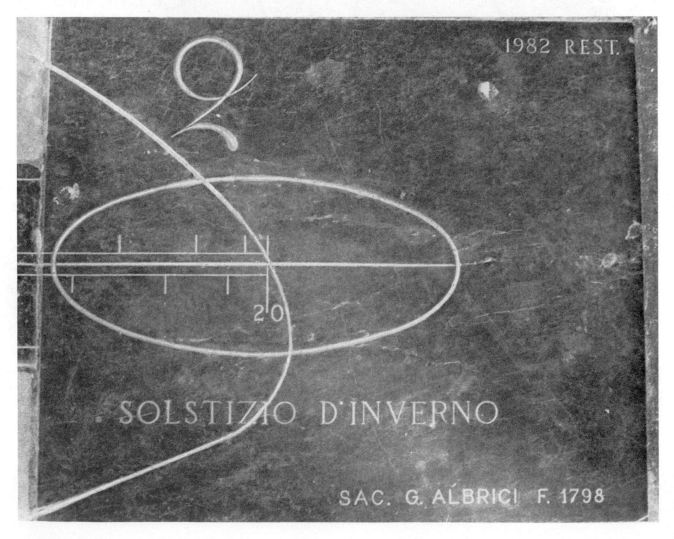

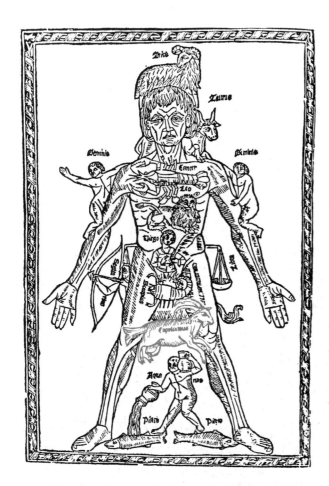

legged, with a serpentine tail. The zodiac in the Baptistry of Florence presents a two-legged goat with a long serpentine tail which curves twice (Fig. 144), while the interesting woodcut of *c.* 1520 represents Capricorn with a knot in its tail, which is tipped with a vestige of the fish-tail, topped with two stars (Fig. 138). This last image is remarkably close to the Capricorn in the antique planisphere of Figure 17.

The contrast between the linear conscious life of the Capricorn and the curvilinear 'hidden life-force' of the unconscious within (which he seeks to keep battened down) is told in the Greek myth of

because of his fear of the life-forces within, which he feels he cannot control or discipline. Some stories derived from Greek mythology trace the tail of the Capricorn image to a dolphin, for it was this human-like fish which was placed in the heavens by the sea-god Poseidon, as a constellation, and given the head of an antelope.

The occultist Blavatsky writes at length on the meaning of the image of Capricorn, pointing out that the word in Sanskrit (*Makaram*) is sometimes wrongly translated as meaning 'crocodile', though really the creature is more of a sea-dragon: it is perhaps this symbolism which has survived into the twelfth-century roundel of the Susa zodiac 'Chapricornus', for a winged dragon is common enough in art, but a winged Capricorn is rare indeed. Indications of the link between Capricorn and the dragon have not disappeared altogether, even in popular zodiacal imagery, for the ruler of

143 (above). Capricorn on the 'zodiacal arch' of the twelfth-century Sacra di San Michele, Val di Susa.

144 (right). Capricorn, with horns, beard and long tail, from among the zodiacal roundels in the thirteenth-century zodiac of the Baptistry of St. John in Florence.

how the Earth-god Pan was pursued by Typhon, and sought to escape by jumping into the Nile. His upper body turned into a goat, while the lower part turned into a fish, and it was in this form that he was transformed by Jupiter into a constellation, safe in the skies. A story which shows how Capricorn was formed from the fear of a spermatic Earth god (Pan) who jumped into water to save himself is a fitting analysis of the deeper nature of the Capricornian personality – for all too often the ambitious goat seeks to distinguish himself merely

Capricorn is the planet Saturn, and many of the pictures which show this classical god being drawn in state portray the beasts pulling the chariot as dragons (Fig. 145).

In the esoteric tradition Capricorn is sometimes called the 'gate of death', for the Cancer–Capricorn axis in the horoscope is mysterious connected with Birth and Death respectively. The idea is that prior to birth the incarnating soul descends through the planetary spheres, drinking in from each the qualities of the respective planets, and is then born into the Earth after leaving the lowest planetary sphere, that of the Moon, the ruler of Cancer. Death itself is linked with Capricorn, not merely because the occultists visualize the deceased as travelling back through the planetary spheres until they reach the outer sphere of Saturn (Fig. 146), but because it is believed that

145. Saturn, devouring his own child, his carriage drawn by dragons. The wheels of the chariot contain the images for the signs over which he used to have rule, Capricorn and Aquarius.

123

146. Medieval representation of the planetary spheres, with Astronomy presiding over the macrocosmic man. Saturn (the sphere of the Thrones) is the planetary sphere contained within the concentric next to that containing the fixed stars. This outermost of the planetary spheres marks the end of time.

time ends at Capricorn. This is one reason why the planetary ruler of Capricorn was sometimes called 'Chronos', for this is the Greek word for Time. It is almost certainly this belief which explains why the San Miniato zodiac, set in the nave pavement (Fig. 147), is so orientated that the Capricorn–Cancer axis lies directly down the nave of the church – after entering the church door, one passes through death towards birth (that is, towards life) in the direction of the altar, where the true Life of Christ is found. One may easily understand why Blavatsky writes that Capricorn is 'now the most sacred and mysterious of the signs of the Zodiac'.

A Famous Zodiac – San Miniato al Monte

Without doubt, the most extraordinary zodiac in Europe is that found in the church of San Miniato al Monte, in Florence (Fig. 82). It represents the earliest known attempt to present a complete programme of symbolic forms derived from astrological and zodiacal lore, in which the pagan lore is placed entirely at the service of Christian symbolism.

The circle of the zodiac itself is almost 3 m (9.8 ft) in diameter, constructed from marble, and is set in the floor of the church (Fig. 147). It is probably the largest circular marble zodiac in Europe, and it is certainly the only one which bears a date, for in a nearby Latin inscription, also set into the pavement, we find the Roman numerals for 1207 recorded, and the zodiac referred to as a 'celestial image'. Considering its great age, and considering the fact that worshippers and visitors to this lovely church are still permitted to walk over

it, the zodiac is in a fairly good state of preservation: the image for Cancer shows a certain amount of patching, while Aquarius is to some extent disfigured.

The twelve symbols are standard medieval images, with the animals portrayed rampant (Fig. 53), Virgo as a woman holding a distaff, Libra also in the form of a woman holding a diminutive pair of scales, Sagittarius as a centaur-horseman, and Capricorn as a goat-fish. The most distinctive of the twelve images is that for Pisces, which is portrayed as a pair of fishes in parallel – thus dispensing with the standard astrological symbolism which was established in antiquity (see p. 140).

In fact, this curious form for Pisces is echoed in the symbolism of the church, in a complex programme of Christian symbolism which need not concern us here. A pair of upright fishes are found on either side of the entrance to the

148. The image of the right-hand fish on the side of the doorway in the upper part of the basilica of San Miniato al Monte, Florence. This fish is related to Pisces, and is an important part of the esoteric symbolism of this church.

raised choir (Fig. 148), and no doubt carry the associations with the symbolism which links the fish with Christ (see p. 143). In being invited to walk between the two fishes, we are being invited to enter into the body of Christ, or even into the new Age of Pisces.

One of the most noteworthy things about the San Miniato zodiac is that it has at its centre the image of a twelve-rayed Sun (Fig. 84), which, to some extent, reminds us of the symbolism of another thirteenth-century zodiac in the Baptistry in Florence (Fig. 82). The presence of the Sun in the centre of the zodiac points to a complex symbolism, one level of which is distinctly Christian, for Christ was often viewed as being the Sun surrounded by the twelve disciples (that is, the twelve signs of the zodiac), and one of the few complex circular zodiacs from antiquity (Fig. 20) actually reflects this notion in portraying a nimbus-rayed human being in the centre of the zodiacal circle.

In the case of the San Miniato zodiac, however, the solar symbolism is a little deeper than usual for it is also reflected in the design of the church itself. Periodically (twice a year, but only for a few seconds during those times) beams of sunlight fall on to certain symbols within the church, and represent certain ideas which are linked at once with Christian doctrine and with medieval astrological theory. For example, the fact that between 7 and 9 March and 6 and 8 October each year a beam of a sunbeam, directed through an upper clerestory window, falls upon the fish upon the choir wall (Fig. 149) is linked with the idea of Christ as a Sun-being, as a sacred fish, and as a representative of the Age of Pisces.

There is considerable evidence to suggest that this date refers not only to the construction of the zodiac (and to the considerable rebuilding of the church) but also to the actual foundation chart of San Miniato, for in that year there was an extraordinary configuration of planets – an event which is still recorded within the fabric of the church. On 28 May 1207 there were no fewer than five planets gathered in the constellation of Taurus: these were the Sun, Moon, Mercury, Venus and Saturn. The importance of Taurus to the symbolic programme of San Miniato is attested in the fact that it is the arc of Taurus in the marble zodiac (Fig. 53) which is aligned to the centre of the arc of sunrise over Florence. The complex symbolism of the various beams of light, daily sunrise points, and other astrological or zodiacal imagery in this extraordinary church has recently been dealt with in considerable depth by Fred Gettings, in his *The Secret Zodiac*, 1987.

149. A shaft of sunlight which falls perfectly twice a year upon the fish on the choir wall is linked with the idea of Christ as a Sun-being. San Miniato al Monte, Florence.

The Age of Aquarius

The vernal point, from which the beginning of the zodiac is measured, in the first degree of Aries, retrogrades through the constellations, and completes a circuit of the skies every 52,920 years. The time during which this point is retrograding through each sign of the zodiac is called an 'Age', and lasts for 2,160 years. At present it is believed by many that we are about to enter, or have just entered, the Age of Aquarius, the vernal point having retrograded through Pisces during the centuries after the birth of Christ. There is no agreement among astrologers as to when one Age ends and the next begins: some claim that the Age of Aquarius began in 1962, but others maintain that it will not begin until the year 2377: there are many other alternatives offered by various schools of astrology.

If we assume that the esoteric tradition is correct, and the birth of Jesus corresponded with the Age of the Fish (see the section on Pisces, page 140), then the Age of Aquarius is unlikely to begin until about 2140. There is not even much agreement as to what the Age of Aquarius will herald – some astrologers speak of the freedom, humanitarianism, and scientific interests of the sign finding expression during that Age. Others, however, mindful of the fact that the ruling planet, Uranus, is a revolutionary and disruptive influence, are less optimistic about the promise of the Age, which will see many changes on the Earth and in the nature of Man.

Among the more memorable images relating to Aquarius and the notion of humanitarian principles associated with the coming Age, is the collection of early horoscopes for the Declaration of American Independence, several of which link the newly formed country

150. Engraving emblematic of the Declaration of Independence, from Ebenezer Sibly's *The Celestial Science of Astrology or Complete Illustration of the Occult Sciences*, 1790. The horoscope on the scroll in the skies is one of several related to this important moment, which is seen by many as a portent of the coming Age of Aquarius.

with the sign Aquarius. The most famous of these images is that engraved for Ebenezer Sibly (Fig. 150). The Tarot card of Temperance (Fig. 151) has been linked with the constellation Aquarius. However, although this image does proclaim a certain duality, the informed symbolist cannot but lament this particular association, for, in truth, the card has its origins in a quite different, non-astrological imagery. One cannot help feeling that a more appropriate Tarot equivalent would have been the seventeenth in the series, 'The Star' (Fig. 152), which has the liquid running to earth, rather than being circulated.

151 (far left). The major arcanum of 'Temperance' from the Tarot cards. The female in the image is recirculating the water rather than distributing it, and this alone indicates that it should not be linked with Aquarius.

152 (left). The major arcanum of 'The Star' from the Tarot cards. The female in the image is pouring the waters as a free gift to Earth: this makes the card a far more satisfactory analogy with the Aquarian impulse.

≈ AQUARIUS

The standard image for Aquarius is of a human-being pouring water from a vase (Fig. 153), and the Latin-derived name means literally 'Water-pourer': this standard figure is extremely close to the Egyptian image (Fig. 34), which portrays a god (sometimes interpreted as a representative of Hapi, the Nile god) pouring not one, but two streams of water. The mystical element in the image is traditionally supposed to be linked with the nature of the 'water', which is more of a life-force than an ordinary liquid – the duality points to the fact that life-forces may be used for both evolutionary or involutionary purposes. Even the early Arabian zodiacs, which omitted the human being (because of the interdiction on using the human figure in art) emphasized the water – a precious enough commodity in the desert, in any case – and the duality, by representing the constellation as a mule carrying a pair of water-barrels. In medieval times we find the 'water' being associated with the mystical dew of the alchemists – the same 'Ros' (the Latin for 'dew') from which some suggest the mystical word 'Rosicrucian' was derived, thus linking the sign with the Christian hermetic tradition. In spite of the importance of water in the associations of both name and tradition, a few images portray Aquarius as an urn only, sometimes even without a stream of life-giving water, as for example in the melothesic image of Figure 19, in which the water-urn is pictured upside down.

In mythological accounts of the zodiacal signs one finds the waters linked with the Nile, to the extent that the standard sigil for the sign is said to have been originally a drawing of the Nilotic waters. However, the Aquarian tradition is far older in Bab-

ylonian astrology, and it has been pointed out by Allen, in *Star-Names and Their Meanings* that in the ancient 'Epic of Creation', the constellation was called Shabatu, 'the Curse of Rain', to which it belongs as the eleventh book, corresponding to the eleventh zodiacal constellation, each of the books corresponding numerically to the other zodiacal figures. The Akkadian 'Ku-ur-ku' meant 'Seat of the Flowing Waters', while the alternative 'Rammanu' meant 'God of the Storm'.

153 (opposite). Image of Aquarius, from the fifteenth-century frescoes in the Salone at Padua.

154 (above). Aquarius standing on the streams of his own liquid, from the thirteenth-century zodiacal cycle on the façade of Amiens cathedral.

155. A fifteenth-century woodcut, an illustration from an edition of Hyginus' *Poeticon Astronomicon*, showing the constellation of Aquarius.

156. Image of Aquarius from the thirteenth-century marble zodiac in the Baptistry of St. John in Florence. The two streams of water appear to be linked with the double stream in the Egyptian tradition.

157. Roundel for Aquarius, the water-pourer, from the marble floor in Canterbury cathedral. There is no doubt a symbolism in the fact that the water starts out in a multi-current stream but by the time it has curled back over the figure, to touch its back, there is only one current left.

The sigil for Aquarius has been traced back to an Egyptian origin, in which there were three zig-zag lines, rather than the modern two. The polymath Athanasius Kircher, who attempted to decipher the Egyptian hieroglyphics, came to the conclusion that the sigil portrayed milk streams (though, of course, this milk was of an esoteric kind), and even made a graphic connection between the sigil and the milk-streams emerging from the multi-breasted goddess, whom he links with the name 'Canopus', but who is really a form of Diana (Fig. 35). The form of the lines has been variously explained: some Theosophist astrologers link the zig-zags with the mystical 'fohat', which is a sort of universal electricity, while other interpreters suggest that it portrays the universal life-force, which is very much the same thing. Almost all are agreed, however, that the lines do not merely represent water. The medieval image of Aquarius at Amiens (Fig. 154) portrays the water-pourer standing on the waves of the water which are streaming (apparently endlessly) from his vase. This is almost certainly intended to show that he is dealing with something other than or-dinary water, for it is both endless and a 'support' for the human being. The Hyginus woodcut of Figure 155 emphasizes the magical nature of the water stream by depicting twelve stars along the liquid flow: in early Greek times this flow of stars was actually called 'Water', and 'Outpouring', and in modern astrology the title has been used to designate a single red star (the modern 'lambda') within the flow. In reality, the stars of Aquarius are not so distinct as those of most of the other zodiacal constellations, and those in the stream are weakest of the entire figure.

We have noted that the Egyptian Aqua-rian figure is male, and that he pours two streams of water from either hand. Curi-ously enough, some of the crude woodcuts do portray Aquarius as pouring two streams of liquid – in almost all such images, the double-stream is a conscious or unconscious throwback to the double-stream of Hapi. However, the only esoteric-based zodiacal figure to show a double-stream is the marble zodiac of the Baptistry in Florence, which portrays a somewhat dramatic Aquarius with two distinct streams (Fig. 156). The esotericism of the double-stream has found its way into poetry, for the poet Keats recognized the magical nature of the liquid in his verses in 'Endymion':

Crystalline brother of the belt of heaven,
Aquarius! to whom King Jove has given
Two liquid pulse-streams 'stead
of feathered wings.   (Book IV, 1, 581 ff)

The Crystalline refers to the 'crystalline sphere' against which the constellations were supposed to be set, and from which the male figure was born. The belt of heaven is, of course, the zodiac itself. The two liquid pulse-streams refer (one supposes) not to anything visible in the skies, or to the standard image of Aquarius, which gen-erally pours a single stream from a single urn, but to the esoteric image, derived from the Egyptian zodiac. This is not unreason-able, as the poet Keats was well-versed in occult and mythological lore. The esot-ericism in the poetic reference is linked with the notion that the two streams, which are being poured to the Earth for the good of humanity, are the transformation of the feathered wings, which Aquarius might have used for his own flight – in other words, the image of Aquarius is the image of the celestial god who chose to sacrifice certain things which might have supported his own development in order that mankind might be helped towards evolution. Another interesting example of the use of specific numbers of streams in the Aquarian image is the marble roundel from Canterbury cathedral (Fig. 157), which starts out as a series of many streams, yet curls back over the figure, in a most unnatural way, to touch the tip of the water-pourer's head in a single stream – perhaps a reference to the one God presiding over the multiplicity of things.

In the Greek mythology Aquarius (already ancient, and well-established in Babylonian astrology, though under different names) was represented by Ganymedes, son of Tros, who was carried to heaven by an eagle on the orders of Jupiter, who (in some versions) wished to retain the child as a cup-bearer, in which capacity one of his duties was to oversee the annual flooding of the Nile. In modern times, since the ancient rulership of Saturn over Aquarius (Fig. 158) has been dispensed with, and the strange Uranus put in its place, the sign has been linked with flight. Perhaps, therefore, there is something prophetic in the Greek mythology, and in the image of Ganymedes, which portrays the child urinating in fear – in such pictures the notions of a flight, of a magical discharge of water, and of the involvement of the gods, are combined. The interesting thing is that while the image of Aquarius is usually interpreted as portraying a gift to mankind (the gift of a life-force, no less) the Grecian origin of the myth suggests that Jupiter had Ganymedes carried away from the Earth because he entertained an unnatural passion for the child – which is why the incident is often referred to as the 'Rape of Ganymedes'. The dualism inherent in this contrast of symbols is a reflection of the dualism of the sign itself, which we shall eventually note.

For all meaning of its name, Aquarius belongs to the Air element, and denotes a nature which is artistic, tenacious and intuitive. Within the nature of the type we find the same duality as exists in the double stream of Hapi, for the temperament is at once peaceful and optimistic, yet also unexpectedly erratic and perverse – perhaps the natural outpouring of its independence and originality. One cannot help feeling that the duality of the streams, hinted at in certain zodiacal images (Fig. 156), is a reference to the dual nature of the Aquarian native, who is at once friendly, humanitarian (giving the water to the human race, so to speak), yet at the same time distant, as though caught up in the remoteness which is one of the soul-conditions of those who dwell for too long in the realm of Ideas (which is another term for the Air world). It is this last characteristic which explains the Aquarian interest in thought, inventiveness, in literature and science. The dualism inherent in the sign has not escaped the attention of modern astrologers, and it has been observed that the blue of the skies, which is 'caused' by our seeing light against the blackness of outer space (that is, by our eyes combining the two extreme contrasts of dualism) is also the blue of Aquarius. It was no accident that the Royal Air Force should adopt the same blue for its uniform, as this Force is itself ruled by Aquarius by virtue of its association with aviation.

Saturnus

158. Personification of Saturn, the planetary ruler (in traditional astrology) over Aquarius and Capricorn. In modern astrology Aquarius is ruled by Uranus.

The Silver Cord

The cord in the image of the fish, sometimes called the 'silver cord', is probably derived from the constellation image, for the weak line of stars, known to the Arabian astrologers as 'Al Risha' (the Cord – Fig. 159), was recognized even by the Babylonians, who called it 'Riksu', which meant the same thing. The imaginary cord may be traced in the constellation from the upper 'fish', straggling downwards to cross the ecliptic, to touch the pale green and blue stars Al Risha (alpha, in the modern astronomical system), before returning upwards, across the vernal point to rejoin the stars marking the body of the other 'fish'.

Whatever the origin of this cord, it has been adopted by the esotericists as representative of an occult symbolism. The idea is that the two fishes, because they swim in opposite directions, are representative of spirit and soul, which do not desire the same things. The spirit yearns for the body-free conditions of Heaven, while the soul, attracted by the pull of the lower desires to the world of the body, has become appetitive for the material things of the Earth. Yet it is a fact that, during life on Earth, the spirit and soul are inexorably linked together, and it is the Nodus, or silver cord, which denotes this connection. Whether the human being will aspire to Heaven, or will desire earthly things, seems to depend upon his relationship to Pisces (that is, in an esoteric context, in his relationship to Christ, of whom Pisces is the zodiacal representative). This probably explains why the image for Pisces is so often found as decorative elements on the façades of churches which display no other zodiacal imagery, as for example at the Norman church at

159. An early Arabian image of the constellation of the Fishes, with the cord well marked.

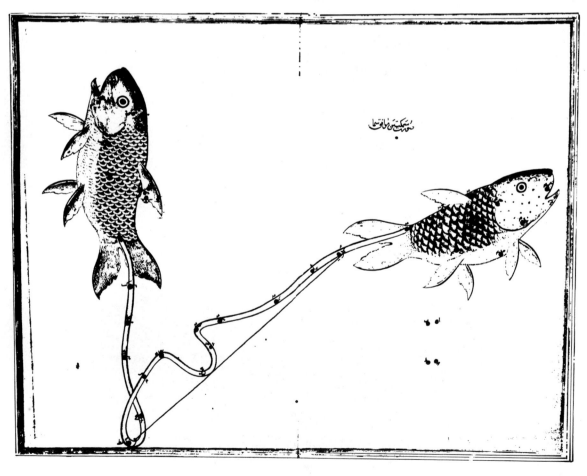

Kilpeck, Hereford and Worcester, which has Piscean imagery on the south door (Fig. 160) and on the northern wall (Fig. 161).

The cxpression of this idea of the 'silver cord' is usually traced to Theosophical literature, and is therefore not much over a century old – however, the idea of the two fishes symbolizing spirit and soul is far older, and is found even in seventeenth-century alchemical texts (Fig. 162).

160 (far left). The image of Pisces on the south door of Kilpeck church, Hereford and Worcester. Twelfth century.

161 (left). The image of Pisces on the north wall of Kilpeck church, Hereford and Worcester. Eleventh century.

162 (below). Fishes of spirit and soul. From an alchemical text after Lambsprinck's *De Lapide Philosophico*, 1677.

♓ PISCES

163. Image of Pisces, from the stained glass 'zodiacal window' in the south wall of Chartres cathedral. Fourteenth century.

The standard image for Pisces is that of two fishes, swimming in opposite directions, their mouths joined by a thread (Fig. 163). The numerous images of Pisces which are found on churches and cathedrals, all emphasize this duality, and the connecting thread, as for example on the façade of Notre Dame (Fig. 164), Sacra di San Michele (Fig. 165) and on the planisphere carried by Atlas in the ornamental gardens of Castle Howard (Figs. 166 and 167).

Designers of zodiacs are usually at great pains to preserve the tradition of the 'duality' of the fishes, and the esoteric nature of the cord – yet, as with all zodiacal images, we do find interesting deviations from this tradition (Fig. 168). While the thread is of great importance to the esoteric symbolism of Pisces, it is sometimes omitted – especially so in modern images in those cases where the deeper symbolism of the zodiac is no longer appreciated. Two

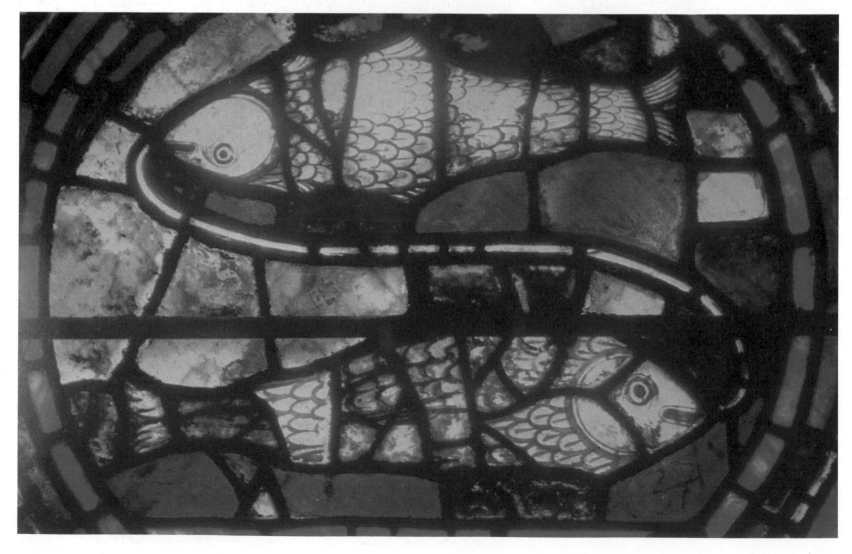

woodcut of Figure 171, for the fin of the top fish touches the back of the lower one. The sixteenth-century painting of the melothesic man in Figure 142 is linked with the esoteric tradition, as we have already noted on p. 120: we should therefore not be surprised to find something special about the handling of Pisces, which is represented as a pair of kissing fishes, nose to nose.

164 (left). Image of Pisces with the cord, set in a spandrel on the façade of the cathedral of Notre Dame, Paris.

165 (below). Image of Pisces from the twelfth-century constellational arch in the Sacra di San Michele, Val di Susa.

interesting medieval exceptions are still found in Italy – the pair of upright fishes in the San Miniato zodiac (Fig. 169) are neither conjoined by a thread, nor swim in opposite directions. This particular symbolism has been shown to be linked with the arcane symbolism of the whole church, however, and so we might say that the exception proves the rule (see p. 126). In the baptistry at Parma is one of the rare upright sculptures by the medieval sculptor Antelami, which shows the seasons or 'labours', the one linked with Pisces actually portraying the pair of fishes without the distinguishing cord (Fig. 170): there appears to be no explanation for this omission, however. In passing, we note that the fins of the fishes touch, so that we might assume that this proximity is intended to represent the sense of spirituality which is conveyed in the notion of the Cord. Another example of this, from a later medieval source, is the pair of pike-like fishes in the sixteenth-century

166. Image of Pisces on the celestial globe carried by Atlas, in the fountain in the gardens of Castle Howard, North Yorkshire. The design is probably early nineteenth century.

The sigil for Pisces is derived from ancient Egyptian sources, and unlike some of the modern sigils for the other zodiacal signs, has come down to modern times in a form which could well be identified by the ancients: the Greek form for Pisces was almost certainly intended to denote the bodies of the two fishes, and the only change to this sigil, introduced in the fourteenth or fifteenth century, was for the connecting line (the Nodus) to be drawn across them, to give the familiar symbol of a 'united duality' which is, in sum, the nature of Pisces itself, being a sign which unites spirit with soul in a form which encourages artistic activity and sensitivity.

Pisces is the last of the Water signs, and the influence is sympathetic, imaginative, suggestible, emotionally malleable, self-indulgent and sentimental. When the energies are disciplined – which is rarely the case – then the native may give direction to this extreme sensitivity, and find a means of expression in poetry, painting or dance. Under pressure, the native gives way to insecurity, and the tendency is to become lazy, restless, chaotic, dreamy and lacking in self-reliance. Much of the 'watery', or dreamy nature, of the sign appears to be derived from its ruling planet, Neptune. In modern astrology the older rulership of Jupiter (Fig. 128) has given way to that of the 'new' planet Neptune, which is highly sensitive, linked in some curious way with liquids, drugs and poisons, with deceit and misunderstandings, and yet is so impressionable, so much in contact with the higher spiritual realm, that it often marks an artistic trend in the horoscope.

The fishes of Pisces in Christian art have their own power of symbolism, mainly because the fish was from very early times

167. Detail of Pisces from the globe in Figure 166.

adopted as a symbol for Christ, and was linked in the secret tradition with the 'Age of Pisces' (see p. 140). Whether this Christian fish was a 'secret' symbol or not is open to question, but when St. Augustine recorded a Greek acrostic verse, said to come from the sacred writings of the Sibyls, in which the name of the fish was secretly linked with a phrase descriptive of Christ, he was merely repeating something already old. The phrase, recorded in his 'City of Gold', is 'Iesous Xristos THeou EUios Soter', the capital letters of which

143

170. The labour of the Month, with the image of Pisces above the head of the labourer. Sculpture attributed to the thirteenth-century mason Antelami, in the Baptistry, Parma.

consequence of their sin.

One of the most mysterious images of Pisces is that found on the façade of the thirteenth-century basilica of San Miniato al Monte, within which church is found a huge marble zodiac (see p. 126). This small detail, scarcely visible from the ground level (Fig. 173), portrays two mermen eating fishes. While few would deny that this is a Piscean symbol, some interpreters view it

as a reference to the Eucharist, claiming that the mermen are, in effect, eating the body of the Fish-King, who is Christ. Others see the fish as symbol of the Piscean mysteries within the church itself.

Set among the cluster of columns on the north portal of the west-front of Chartres cathedral is a tiny image of a mermaid grasping two fishes (Fig. 174) which are again facing in the same upright direction,

seind vil kündig . Das zeychen ist tzüge
dem planeten Jupiter mitt seiner natu

Sangwineo.

Von dem fis

¶ Der fisch hat
menschen gelyder
gar hynab vñ jre
tagen. Weñ der 1
dem fisch ist daz g
hat über dz teyl 6
trio od Nordes. d
wasser flegma v
natur ist. so ist gü
frawen neme vñ

schafft zwischen den leüten mache. nei
schlahen. gold vñ silber wäschen. vnd
dz güt thün das zü wasser gehöret. vñ
müß mit wasser volbracht werden . al
mülen mache oder auff dem wasser far
sunderlich gegen dem teyl Septentri
gut ertzneyen vñ kauffmanschatz treyb

171. Pike-like fish from
a German astrological
text of the late
fifteenth century.

172. Font, with fishes: one of the most enduring symbolical links between Christ, the fishes of Pisces and water. From the cathedral museum, Orvieto.

yet not joined by the cord: since the astrological symbolism at Chartres is linked with an esoteric tradition (see p. 140), we may take it that the images of upright fishes are an occult device intended to point to some hidden meaning within the design of the zodiac or building in which the images appear. The formal image for Pisces was never located with the other zodiacal images on the portal at Chartres, but was represented as a single fish on the southern portal of the same front (Fig. 175), below the image of Gemini. Quite unesoteric is the triad of fishes, meant to represent Pisces, on

173. Detail of the thirteenth-century façade of the basilica of San Miniato al Monte, Florence. The centre relief portrays two mermen devouring fishes.

174. Detail on the façade of Chartres cathedral, showing a mermaid holding two fishes – part of the zodiacal symbolism.

the Sun Alliance building in London's Cheapside (Fig. 176): we may presume that the use of three fishes, and the omission of the cord, arises from ignorance, rather than from any wish to denote an arcane line of thought. Oddly enough, even this has its medieval prototype in the curious French woodcut of Figure 177. This triad breaks all the rules, for the fishes point in the same direction, and do not have a connecting cord: the straight line emerging from the mouth of the central fish has nothing to do with the cord which joins the two fishes in traditional images, but (as the text makes clear) is actually intended to denote the path of the Sun, the line of the ecliptic.

One of the strangest images for Pisces, in a symbolism which has not yet been explained, is that found on the pagan zodiac which shows the sign as a fish in the mouth of a fish-tailed creature, much like a version of Capricorn.

175 (below left). Single fish as symbol of Christ, on the south portal of the western façade of Chartres cathedral. This symbol, with that for Gemini above it, is separated from the other ten zodiacal symbols, which are on the archivolts of the northern portal of the same western façade.

176 (left). Modern symbol for Pisces, which shows a break with tradition by depicting three fishes. From the series of zodiacal images on the façade of the Sun Alliance Insurance building in Cheapside, London.

177. Medieval zodiac with three fishes as a symbol of Pisces. The line emerging from the mouth of the central fish has nothing to do with the silver cord but is a representation of the ecliptic, the apparent path of the Sun through the centre of the zodiacal belt.

Astrological Sites

The European cathedral-builders of the thirteenth and fourteenth century were deeply influenced by the 'new' astrological lore which was flooding into Europe from the Arabian astrology, by way of the new translations which were being made, in Spain and England. The result of this is that many of the surviving cathedrals of France, England and Italy are redolent with astrological symbols. The most famous cathedrals in France – Notre Dame, in Paris (Fig. 178) and Chartres, to the north-west of Paris – have as their central Christian symbolism a complex system of astrological and alchemical lore. Samples of images from these two buildings are given in Figures 89, 125 and 163.

In particular, Chartres cathedral is rich in zodiacal imagery. Without doubt, the most famous zodiacal images are the beautifully coloured roundels (south transept, south wall) of the zodiacal images, of which the image for Pisces is perhaps the most lovely (Fig. 163). The most important of the zodiacal series at Chartres evince esoteric use of symbolism, as may be expected of a place steeped in mysticism, occultism and esoteric lore: this is the zodiacal series and sequences on the western façade of the cathedral.

The Royal Portal, constructed in the twelfth century, was probably intended as an inner narthex portal on the lines of Vezelay (see p. 114). Each of the three portals contains zodiacal symbolism, but only the two outer ones are involved in the use of secret zodiacal symbolism. The inner portal shows Christ in glory, within a mandorla, surrounded by the standard symbols of the zodiacal symbols of the Evangelists (Fig. 119): to the right of Christ is the Aquarius of Matthew and the Leo of Mark, to His left is the Scorpionic eagle of John and the Taurus of Luke.

The zodiacal imagery of the north portal is set out in the following sequence (alternating with the 'labours of the months') in the archivolts starting bottom left:

April, ARIES (inner); July, CANCER (outer); May, TAURUS (inner); August, LEO (outer); September, VIRGO.

This arrangement completes the upward movement of the symbols, so that Virgo is at the top of the portal, as might be expected in a cathedral dedicated to the Virgin Maria. The sequence from the bottom right of the opposite archivolt ends in the sequence of Sagittarius which confronts Virgo across the top of the archivolt:

January, CAPRICORN (inner); October, LIBRA (outer); November, SCORPIO (inner); February, AQUARIUS (outer); December, SAGITTARIUS.

The sequence is clearly intended to be read in terms of left and right, with the images for Aries to Virgo on the left-hand side of the archivolt, and Libra to Aquarius on the right-hand side of the archivolt. This complexity of forms may appear to be designed to give Virgo the ascendancy because of the dedication – however, it does not explain why Sagittarius should be opposite to Virgo, save perhaps in reference to the Knights Templar who are associated with both the funding and the building of Chartres. The complexity of the arrangement has obscured from most art historians and occultists the fact that the zodiacal

178. The cathedral of
Notre Dame, Paris –
the centre of medieval
astrological and
alchemical lore.

179. Libra roundel from the thirteenth-century marble pavement in Canterbury cathedral.

Christian image of Pisces as Christ. Gemini is expressed as the image of two knights standing behind a single shield which points down to a single fish (Fig. 175). This fish is at once Pisces and a symbol of Christ (see p. 126). The double-knight image of Gemini is to be linked with the Knights Templar on the grounds that the Seal of the order represents two knights in armour riding a single horse.

On the same north portal a number of zodiacal images have been carved into roundels on the clusters of columns. Especially beautiful are the images for Scorpio and Pisces (Fig. 174). However, the quality of the work would suggest that these images are late restorations, and it would therefore be foolish to derive too many conclusions about the interesting details of symbolism contained within these images.

Inside the cathedral south transept (south wall) is the so-called 'Zodiac Window', which presents the twelve signs of the zodiac in stained-glass medallions, alongside the corresponding 'labours of the months', which are not identical with those set out on the portal sculptures. January, with three heads to represent past, present and future, is with Aquarius. February, a hooded man in front of a fire, is with Pisces. March, a man pruning a vine, is with Aries. April, with spring flowers, is with Taurus. May, a hawking Knight, is with Gemini. June, a man cutting grass, is with Cancer. July in the figure of a reaper, is with Leo. August as a thresher of corn, is with Virgo. September, treading grapes, is with Libra. October, casking wine, is with Scorpio. November, symbolized as a man killing a pig, is with Sagittarius. December, a scene of feasting, is with Capricorn. Without

sequence is incomplete. The images for Gemini and Pisces are missing from this zodiacal symbolism. That they are intentionally excluded is clearly expressed in the chaotic arrangement of this archivolt, for Gemini is ruled by Mercury and Pisces is ruled by Jupiter – these two planets are also the rulers of the images at the top of the archivolt (namely Virgo and Sagittarius). The two missing images are found on the north arch of the Royal Portal, in an arrangement which (it has been shown) is designed to express esoteric symbolic forms linked with the Knights Templar and the

154

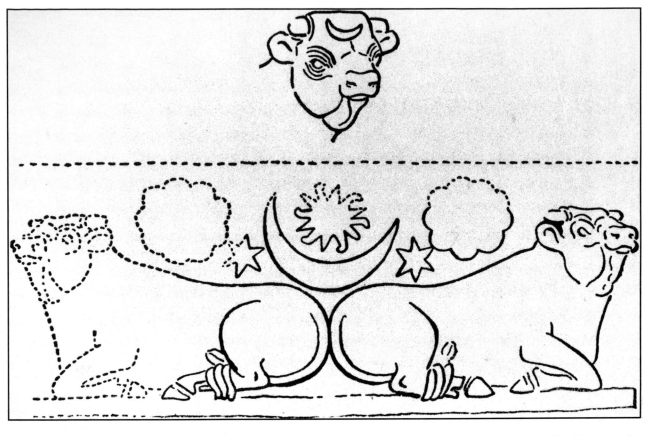

exception, the images for this zodiacal series are standard medieval in form and symbolism.

In England are two zodiacal extremes – one of the oldest zodiacal remains, and the most impressive of modern zodiacs. The oldest in England is that in Canterbury, set in the marble pavement of the Trinity Chapel in the cathedral as part of a rich mosaic of symbolism. Most of the twelve roundels are still visible, yet the majority are badly defaced, set among the roundels for the 'twelve labours' and the corresponding 'virtues and vices', so important in medieval symbolism. There are many surprises among the symbolism of the zodiacal sections – for example, the roundel which depicts Libra (Fig. 179) contains one of the most secret of all esoteric symbols, the image of the alchemical Quintessence, the magical element which is said to lie just behind the appearance of the familiar physical world, and to maintain its life-forces. This symbol is said to have arrived in the west, for use in magical texts and esoteric architectural details, from the

Middle East: a good example is that in the detail between the two bulls in the lunar 'Bull of Heaven' relief from a steatite bowl (Fig. 180) found during the excavations of the ancient Moon-god temple at Ur, in Babylon.

The most impressive modern zodiac in England is also probably the most remarkable in Europe. This is the zodiac on the façade of Bracken House in Cannon Street, London, which is designed in the tradition of the medieval horlogia, as a huge clock-face set within the circular zodiac (see page 54).

The twelfth-century Canterbury zodiac is probably the only surviving medieval zodiac in England, though there are zodiacal programmes and details of zodiacal symbolism in several British cathedrals and churches. The most famous of the individual zodiacal images are those at Kilpeck, in Hereford and Worcester, where the image for Pisces appears in two separate symbolic forms (Figs. 160 and 161). It is evident that in former times zodiacal imagery appeared with great frequency in ecclesiastical design, but with the loss of the old knowledge of the zodiacal symbolism, the uneasy feeling that the zodiac is somehow pagan, and the state-supported opposition to the earlier Christian imagery fostered before the Reformation, the use has fallen into decline. Evidence of a vast programme of zodiacal images may still be observed on the almost obliterated porch of the now disused church of St. Margaret's in Walmgate, York. This porch is said to have been incorporated into the fabric of St. Margaret's when its original church (that

of St. Nicholas, outside Walmgate Bar) was ruined in the siege of York in 1644. The zodiacal roundels are now so defaced that it requires considerable expertise even to recognize them – however, Moses Cotsworth of York did provide a somewhat clumsy wood engraving (dated 1905) which gives some idea of the original design.

Although few people would recognize the stone circles as 'zodiacal designs', the truth is that many of the larger circles of standing stones in the British Isles are related to the zodiac, in the sense that they are designed

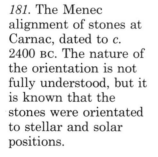

181. The Menec alignment of stones at Carnac, dated to *c.* 2400 BC. The nature of the orientation is not fully understood, but it is known that the stones were orientated to stellar and solar positions.

(among other things) to reveal the important points of sunrise, sunset, moonrise and moonset, over a cycle of years. The circles at Stonehenge and Callanish in the Isle of Lewis, Scotland, have been studied in considerable depth in regard to these orientation lines, and while there is no corresponding zodiacal imagery linked with the circles, it is worth observing that these, as well as the avenues of stones at Carnac in Brittany (Fig. 181) are linked with zodiacal orientation.

There are several individual zodiacal images within the basilica of the Madeleine, at Vezelay, but the most important series is that found on the 'Zodiacal Arch' on the tympanum inside the narthex of the basilica. This arch is usually dated between 1135 and 1130, though it was partly restored by Violet le Duc. The zodiacal images are interspersed with roundels depicting the months, and other medieval symbolic images. The outer circumferencial frieze contains the following sequence, running from left to right, arching over the central figure of Christ the Judge:

January, AQUARIUS, February,
PISCES, March, ARIES, April,
TAURUS, May, Spring, GEMINI, June,
CANCER, (*), Dog, Acrobat, Siren,
LEO, July, VIRGO, August, September,
LIBRA, October, SCORPIO, November,
SAGITTARIUS, Year-end?,
CAPRICORN, December.

At (*), between Cancer and an unidentified image of a dog, is a compressed vesica piscis, a contracted arc, into which is fitted an image of a long-necked bird, here called the 'bird arc', for want of a better name. The

182. The roundel for Capricorn, from the Vezelay zodiac.

sequence of the zodiacal series has been shown to be reflected in the secret geometry of the tympanum.

The curious arrangement (beginning with Aquarius and ending with Capricorn) might be argued as being symbolically linked with the planet Saturn, which had rule over both signs in medieval astrology. This means that the pairs of zodiacal roundels reflect the planetary sequences set out by Ptolemy and Firmicus in their classical texts, rising up the tympanum in the following order:

Moon   – CANCER   Sun – LEO
Mercury – GEMINI and VIRGO
Venus   – TAURUS and LIBRA
Mars   – ARIES and SCORPIO
Jupiter – PISCES and SAGITTARIUS
Saturn   – AQUARIUS and CAPRICORN

With this arrangement, the signs Cancer and Leo are located on the right and left respectively, above the head of Christ, and may be taken to symbolize their rulers the Moon and Sun, which planets are usually

157

figured above the head of the crucified Christ in medieval art. This latter suggestion is confirmed by the curious lunar 'bird arc' which has been inserted between Cancer and the next roundel of the unidentified 'dog' roundel.

Of particular pictorial interest in the zodiacal roundels are Aries and Taurus which are represented in (rare) images terminating in fish-tails, rather like the distinctive roundel for Capricorn (Fig. 182): these are derived from the Arabic manuscript tradition, but may have been adopted by the medieval builders as initiation symbols. Gemini appears to be an image of two dramatically embracing men between two stars (Castor and Pollux?). Were it not for the insistent form of the claws, the image for Cancer might easily be confused with Scorpio. Leo is unique in medieval zodiacal imagery in that it appears to show the lion licking its cub into shape (see p. 80). Virgo holds in each hand flowers and fruit, perhaps vestigial remains of the Spica corn of the constellational image: she wears a distinctive scarf-like maphorion. Libra is male with the balance in his left hand, signalling in recognition to Christ with his right hand. Scorpio is a most curious creature, something like a six-legged camel with an evil-looking tail (Fig. 117). Sagittarius is a centaur, shooting his bow behind him, in the tradition of the constellation images, though he is not cantering, as is so often the case. The distribution of other image-groups has only a peripheral link with astrology.

Among the hermetic bas-reliefs in the three porches of the West front of the cathedral of Amiens are a series of zodiacal and seasonal images, which are said to have been designed by the architect Robert de Luzarches (1236), though it is unlikely that they were cut until the fourteenth century, when the west front was completed. The fourteenth-century zodiacal images are in the north porch, set in the rounded quatrefoils characteristic of these lovely porches. The zodiacal images run at the top of the lower half of the frieze. In the left-hand side of the porch (from the outside, towards the doorway) is the following sequence:

CANCER, LEO, VIRGO, LIBRA, SCORPIO, SAGITTARIUS

On the right-hand side of the porch (from the doorway towards the outside) is the sequence:

CAPRICORN, AQUARIUS, PISCES, ARIES, TAURUS, GEMINI

The images are beautifully preserved, and any symbolic addition is of the most subtle kind. Aries is a ram with curled horns standing against a winter backdrop of two leafless trees. With the next sign Taurus, the traditional bull, the two trees have begun to take leaf: one wonders if the insistent symbol of the three-branched tree immediately behind the bull has any reference to the Cross, for Taurus is sometimes associated with the mithraic bull, which gave its blood in sacrifice for the annual redemption of the world. In Gemini, the two trees are more luxuriant in their foliage: the couple are male and female, holding hands in a most lovely gesture (Fig. 69). Cancer is one of the most lifelike crabs in the whole series of European zodiacs, perfectly placed within the structure of the quatrefoil (Fig. 79). It is no longer possible

183. The image of Capricorn, with his tail to the entrance of Amiens cathedral.

to determine precisely what foliage Virgo holds – perhaps it is a remnant of the corn associated with the asterism. Libra is a female, holding the scales in her right hand. Scorpio has all the appearance of being a Basilisk (Fig. 118), which in medieval iconography was one of the most frequently used symbols for the Devil. Sagittarius is perhaps the most interesting deviant in this series – he is of the Pan-type, rare in zodiacal sculpture, derived from the constellation literature (Fig. 130): he is no longer a horse-man, but has half of his body bestial, with a long tail in the manner of the imagery attached to the god Pan. Such images are found more frequently in the medieval manuscript tradition, however, than on church fabric. Sagittarius is directing his arrow into the church. Capricorn has its fish-tail back to the cathedral, facing as it is in the direction of the zodiacal order (Fig. 183). Aquarius is a partly clothed and bearded man, pouring the waters to his own left: he is standing in the waters which flood the Earth below him. In Pisces it is as though this flood has covered the Earth, for the quatrefoil is unique in this series in being filled with the symbols of the related element of Water. The two fishes themselves swim in opposite directions, and hold the Nodus or silver cord in their mouths.

The sequence of the zodiacal images is perhaps difficult to account for until one realizes that it begins to the left with the sign Cancer ruled by the Moon, and ends to the left with Sagittarius, itself associated with the ninth house of Religion, shooting his arrow into the cathedral nave. The Moon is significant because it is linked with the Virgin Maria (often depicted as sitting or standing on a lunar crescent) as the archetype of womanhood, and of course the cathedral is dedicated to the Virgin. It is little wonder that Capricorn should turn its back from the cathedral, for it is in this sign that Saturn, the polar opposite of the Moon, has his rule. The earthly femininity is represented in Taurus, which ends the sequence, on the right-hand side of the porch: Taurus is ruled by Venus, which female planet is often linked with the Virgin, both in the magic of symbolism and in its numerological aspects.